IN PERENDINUM AEVUM

CARMINA LATINA

Mustela vel potius Telamus

IN PERENDINUM AEVUM

CARMINA LATINA

quae confecit

Stephanus Coombs

… praeter enim visum pertenderit in perendinum aevum
hesterna cantus portio potentis …

evertype
MMXV

Published by Evertype, 73 Woodgrove, Ballyfin Road, Portlaoise, Co. Laois, Ireland. www.evertype.com.

First edition 2015.

A catalogue record for this book is available from the British Library.

ISBN-10 1-78201-106-4
ISBN-13 978-1-78201-106-4

Typeset in Minion Pro and Requiem by Michael Everson, based on a design by Ingela Hallonquist and Stephen Coombs.
Illustrations pp. 189 and 195: Magnus Bäckmark
Photographs, front cover and frontispiece: Ingela Hallonquist
Photographs, Occasiones Servatae: Stephen Coombs

Cover: Michael Everson, based on a design by Ingela Hallonquist and Stephen Coombs.

Printed by LightningSource.

Dispositio codicis

CONTENTS

INDEX CARMINUM

... Grandes iturus ostreas voravi
duodenas labra vino Muscadeti rigans ...

... Conficere hoc velit ars neque conficit ...

Ad J. E. Holmiensem

Me tetigit fulgore brevi tua forma Georgi:
quale fuisset iter deficiente tuo?

Carmina

CITIES

Santiago de Compostela

Field of an ancient star, soaked in an accustomed
holiness that you hardly think worthy of mention,
yesterday evening you resounded
with dancing of countrified modesty;

now in the morning you are awakened
by the cheerful wailings of a bagpiper in your alleys
and the stones under the musicianly feet
have just been washed down and give off new odours;

a youth prepares for visitors the as yet
unopened tavern, sweeps and polishes;
in the markets lobsters are being bought,
beans, thyme, cabbages, duck, goats;

Galician words caress the ear; high on her head
an old woman carries unsteady purchases to her cottage;
soon we will be granted in earthenware cups
the Galician wine we thirst after:

on earth there is no town of livelier merit,
for the cathedral church has nourished
with heavenly bread its citizens in every age
and does not deny crumbs to strangers.

Campus Stellae

Stellae vetustae Campe, sanctitate
saturatus solita quam vix memorandam habes
saltatione rustici pudoris
resonabas here vespere:

nunc angiportis mane suscitant te
hilarantes ululatus utricularii
recensque lauti dant novos odores
lapides sub pede musico:

nondum reclusam praeparat tabernam
peregrinis adulescens, verrit et expolit:
foris emuntur cammari, phaseli,
thyma, caules, anates, caprae:

Gallaeca verba blandiuntur auri:
capite altam dubiam fert mercem anus ad casam:
Gallaeca vina fictili sitita
tribuentur cito vasculo:

tellure non est urbs alacrioris
meriti, nam cathedralis nutriit incolas
aedes superno pane sempiternos
neque micas negat advenis.

Stockholm

I shall be, am and have been without a wife, yet it was
as a home unsure in intimacy, rather like that of a father-in-law,
that Stockholm, polished and richly graceful,
kept moist by the minutest of waves, received me.

What would it matter that a palace were tepid
towards me or warm or coldly inhospitable?
Absolute beauty lived here,
entrancement beggaring dreams.

One who does not ask my loyalty I loyally belay
and cannot easily leave the city of captivation
as I remember the splendid vision,
a unique radiance arisen just once.

Holmia

Mi deerit ac deest defuitque coniunx,
tamen anceps domus usu ceu soceri fere
   undis recepit me madens modestis
      decore uber teres Holmia.

Quid attineret regiam mihi esse
tepidam vel calidam vel frigore inhospitam?
   Hic vixit absoluta pulchritudo,
      lepor orbans ope somnia.

Fidelis insto non fidem roganti
neque possum facile urbem linquere fascini
   cum visionem splendidam recordor,
      semel ortum iubar unicum.

Lisbon

Lisbon prides herself on her black and white paving stones.
The white colour is often very slightly warmed
with the tint of roses or refreshed with gold,
the black is dulled to an ashen tone

under our heels as they disturb the dust –
unless in a flood of rain the streets strewn
with lamps glisten back in the Lusitanian night,
and the stars in the sky are outdone.

Here the very songs are known as fates: in them
dark feelings are inspired by burdensome topics
and luminous feelings by pleasant ones; now hearts
are trodden into the ground, now they shine with joy

until nothing is left of the man detained at sea;
nothing of the woman sorrowing over her lonely state
before the altar of the family gods, or of any living being
in an otherwise wretched condition;

left is only the art of the geometers turned into a melody
of sighing mouths and guitars as it imitates
and in tones converts to measure
the distance between white and black.

The husband has been borne far way from the wife
and she with her memories is hidden far away from him;
so too in the city the peak of the hill from afar
looks down upon the broadening Tagus.

Through the ages distances separate
the least important things of every kind
and all the widespread host of the human beings
we most love. Wise Lisbon, hail!

Olisipo

Nigris superbit tesseris et albis
Olisipo. Color albus saepe minutius
   rosis refotus vel refectus auro,
      hebetatus cinere est niger

sub calce nostra pulverem movente,
nisi fluctu pluviali lampadibus viae
   sparsae renident nocte Lusitana,
      Iovis astris superobrutis.

Hic carmina ipsa fata nuncupantur,
quibus atram gravia afflant grataque candidam
   affectionem: corda proteruntur
      modo, lucent modo gaudio

dum nil relictum sit viri morantis
maribus, nil apud aram sorte Penatium
   sola dolentis feminae secusve
      animantis miserabilis:

relicta tantum est ars geometrarum
melos orum et cithararum facta gementium,
   distantiam inter candidum nigrumque
      imitans et modulans tonis.

Procul maritus latus est marita,
procul uxor reminiscens conditur et viro,
   proculque in urbe despicit cacumen
      ita collis patulum Tagum.

Longinquitates separant per aeva
genere omni minimas res atque hominum gregem
   carissimorum multifariam omnem.
      Olisipo sapiens, ave!

7

Oxford

Once yellowish and now soiled, the diseased stone
of the monuments of Oxford seems hardly
to be perceived by the strange minds
of those intent on something more nebulous.

From time to time, to be sure, it is made free from dirt,
is restored with remedies, is scraped and finds itself
conspicuous, but it ages again by degrees,
imaging the builder in its weaknesses.

Let us carry this idea further: the city continues
to die as it were in the walls of the souls of those
living here, but once formed in them it will endure
for ever, the same albeit in a new form.

The ox does not ford the river Isis twice
without to some extent unexpected experiences,
by which the wet ox is made to gain knowledge
and also the river clinging to the ox.

What is the university's message? That you
should devote yourself to just such things as survive,
that are both ancient and contemporary, genuinely yours
and at the same time the property of your predecessors.

Oxonium

Sufflavus ante, nunc et inquinatus
lapis aeger monumentis Oxoniensibus
    vix mente mira percipi videtur
      meditantis nebulosius.

Subinde sane sorde liberatur,
medicinis reparatur, scalpitur, eminet,
    tamen senescit denuo gradatim,
      simulacrum vitiis fabri.

Quod transferatur: pergit urbs moriri
animarum quasi muris hic habitantium
    at semper illis structa permanebit
      eadem etsi specie nova.

Haud bis vado bos transit Isidem amnem
sine partim necopinis experientiis
    quis cogitur bos humidus doceri
      et inhaerens fluvius bovi.

Quid nuntiatur universitate
studiorum? Modo tali des operam rei
    quae sit superstes, prisca et huius aevi,
      tua vere, veterum simul.

Madrid

There is more heat than Achilles himself could have borne,
yet I am excessively eager for yet more, for it is necessary
to have more and to be more:
Madrid excessively demands more.

San Bernardino makes his way towards you, tavern,
Recio lays claim to you with his name,
and revisiting you I hate the harshness of time passing,
I weep for the impulsive boy of former days:

I lament indiscriminately things mournful and joyful;
your water of life, once the rich fount
of a younger man's inordinate ideas,
fierily consumes the old man too.

Night will bring a cooler temperature, equalling
what perchance would be pleasant enough elsewhere by day.
But in this city everything pleasant disgusts;
may I be burnt more, may I burn more!

Madritum

Plus est caloris quam quod ipse Achilles
tolerasset, tamen ultra plus nimis appeto,
    nam plus necesse habere, plus et esse est:
        Madritum plus nimis exigit.

Popina, Bernardinus appropinquat
tibi Sanctus, Recius te nomine vindicat,
    odique tempus triste te revisens,
        prius acrem puerum fleo:

large lamentor lugubre atque laetum:
aqua vitae tua, quae fons cognitionibus
    exaggeratis iunioris olim
        erat amplus, cremat et senem.

Refrigerabit nox, status caloris
erit aequus sat amoeno forte alibi die.
    Sed displicent hac urbe cuncta amoena:
        magis urar, magis ardeam!

Paris

I was reconnoitring you, city of Paris. Though
the plane tree's branches were letting fall
their emaciated leaves, the air, stirred by the wings
of the west wind, smelt of verdant spring.

You, treasure-house of Gaul, imbue me with hope,
whether it be the hope of eating well
or of taking possession of a rare book beside the Seine;
you make me eager for the best.

Providently you have laid down that there shall be
norms of urbanity and elegance for the nations.
How we need your guiding index finger: or perhaps,
being brought to you for judgement, your thumb!

About to depart I devoured luxurious oysters
by the dozen, moistening my lips with Muscadet.
Just as pearl or mother-of-pearl
or as the bow that accompanies rain

shakes its colours before our eyes; as, say,
the plants in the garden glitter with drops of dew,
or as the glowing opal with its tiny
specks twinkles flutteringly,

with corresponding effect a thousand delicate flavours
with their ever changing subtleties gave pleasure
to this palate of mine, almost that of a glutton
who has been restraining himself for too long.

Having returned home I now watch with pleasure
in a charming film the child dancers of your theatre,
dressed in the colours of the oyster,
and I think of you.

Lutetia Parisiorum

Lutetiam urbem te Parisiorum
speculabar. Cadere etsi frondem aceris macram
   ramus sinebat, ver olebat aër
      viride alis zephyri citus.

Spem, Galliae thesaure, tu mihi indis,
bene seu spes sit edendi, seu prope Sequanam
   inusitatum codicem occupandi:
      avidum me facis optimi.

Urbanitatis elegantiaeque
fore normas statuisti provida gentibus.
   Quantum indigemus indice arbitrante,
      nisi adacti tibi pollice!

Grandes iturus ostreas voravi
duodenas labra vino Muscadeti rigans.
   Ut margarita conchave unionis
      vel ut arcus pluviae comes

suos colores vibrat ante ocellos,
ut in horto puta guttis roris holus nitet
   vel ut sublucet et micat coruscans
      opalus cum minimis notis,

gustus pari vi mille delicati
placuerunt variatis munditiis suis
   paene helluonis huic meo palato
      moderati nimium diu.

Domum regressus nunc tui theatri
pueriles lepidam per pelliculam choros
   quos induebant ostreae colores
      reputans te video libens.

Decent people are supposed to interpret
each body as a useless burden and to prefer
the function known as spirit, which
will have nothing to do with the vulgar atom;

but the body does not recoil from being a body;
it wants to be the master of its master, it cannot
surrender authority, inch by inch
or all at once, to the incompatible spirit.

Dangerous is spring, dangerous is human hope,
the children's dancing is a source of danger,
as are the pleasure of living, our very life,
people, the city; as we are, I and you.

Interpretari corpus omne oportet
reverentes homines ut pondus inutile
et malle munus spiritum vocatum
atomo quod vacet improbo:

sed corpus esse corpus haud recusat:
domino vult dominari, spiritui nequit
auctoritatem dedere unciatim
subitove haud sociabili.

Periculosum ver, periculosa
hominum spes, chorus infans causa periculi,
vitae voluptas, ipsa vita nostra,
homines, urbs: ego, tu sumus.

MOMENTS HELD

Paper and living people! Camera-caught
moments for you to inspect and keep I've brought;
"served ob- and pre-" should be their soubriquet,
ob- now by eyes, pre- for some future day.

OCCASIONES SERVATAE

Charta atque vivi! Quas tueamini
occasiones photographus fero:
    bis more servandae vocentur,
        nunc oculis sed et in futurum.

In Terra Camporum Procul Conspectus Vicus
Mons Alacer

Arces Hispanas res dicimus avias avendas:
    in alterum aevum restat haec quieta:
    loci loquendo sensus haud narrabilis
        redditur igne gelu.

Nullum hominem numeras: praesentia pendet ante mentem
    divina tantum, nec deus sit ille
    quem cor vel intellectus optet persequi:
        est enim omissus ab his

corpora corda animos qui sustinet intimus profundus
    amplectiturque caecus universum,
    fundamen ipsum cognitus fundaminis
        vel deus ipse dei.

In Tierra de Campos the Village of Montealegre
Seen in the Distance

Castles in Spain are what we call things inaccessible and
to be longed for; this one stands set to survive into another age;
a sense of place which speech cannot convey
is turned by fire into ice.

No human beings are there for you to count, only a divine
presence hovering before the mind – and not in the sense
of a god such as heart or understanding would wish to pursue;
for unconsidered by these there is

one who sustains bodies, hearts and minds inwardly, deeply,
and embraces the universe blindly, acknowledged
to be the very foundation of foundation
or as the very god of god.

Os Speluncae Vallensis in Hispania
Septentrionali

Nos tellus cohibet quasi Tartara lumen intuentes
     circumdat asper quod rudisque margo.
  Figura visi plena non discernitur,
        attamen et iuvenes

lumine opinamur medio nimis obrutos nitore
     manuque ductos liberos senesque.
  Specus in ore si manes humanitas
      condita luce patet.

The Mouth of a Cave, the Cueva del Valle,
in Northern Spain

Held in by the earth as if by infernal regions
we gaze at light that is surrounded by a rough, crude border.
The complete shape of what we see cannot be made out,
nonetheless it is young people

we conjecture in the middle of the light, all too struck out
by the brightness, children being led by the hand and old people.
If you stay in the mouth of a cave the human condition is shown
obscured by luminosity.

Linter in Rivo Oxonii

Quae longe distant mihi somnia iam diu iuventae
    origine ipsa non erant propinqua.
  Virens videtur ac smaragdis clarior
    arborea ampla coma,

lenior et speculis aqua limpida sublevat iuventam
    ut flumine arescente sublevaret
  sive ultionis malleus percelleret
    diraque durities:

praeter enim visum pertenderit in perendinum aevum
    hesterna cantus portio potentis.
  O somniorum praevalens vicinitas
    quam valide cupii!

A Punt on the River at Oxford

The dreams of youth, which for me have long been far in the distance,
were not close to me even at the beginning.
Abundant foliage of trees appears greenly alive
and brighter than emeralds,

and limpid water, smoother than mirrors, supports young folk
as it would even if the river dried up,
or if a hammer of revenge struck,
and dreadful hardship,

for yesterday's deal of potent enchantment will have continued
beyond what is seen into the era of the day after tomorrow.
O powerful nearness of dreams, that
which I have mightily desired!

Finis Terrae Gallaecus Mense Augusto MCMLXXVII

Hic finit terram Gallaecia nube comminante.
    Tres pusiones prodeunt repente
et insusurrant exstituram imaginem.
    Carmina consilii

non adhibent tibia mira mihi pervago carenti,
    nec in periclis aucupor Paminam,
sed est locoque horaeque fascinatio
    histrica et apta melo.

Mox potui post hoc, licet addere propter hoc stupere:
    paucis diebus noveram Michaeam
viisque obliquis sum profectus ad scholam
    instituendam alias.

Res vitarum hominum vanescere crederes ut illos:
    at omnia, omnes nexibus ligantur
quos haud mereri clamitem fiduciam
    ipse nisi experiar.

Galician Fisterra/Finisterra, August 1977

Here Galicia sets an end to earth under threatening cloud.
Three small boys suddenly appear and gently suggest
that a picture come into being. Songs of advice
they do not bring to bear on me,

a wanderer lacking any marvellous flute, nor am I in perilous
situations trying to catch Pamina as if she were a bird,
but both the place and the hour hold a magic that is
theatrical and suited to melody.

Soon after this – one might add, because of this – I had reason
to be astounded; within a few days, having made the acquaintance
of Micah, I set out by indirect paths towards the school
which would be established at another time.

You might think the contents of our lives evanish as we do,
but all actions, all people are linked together by connections
which I would not claim to be deserving of trust if I did not
experience them myself.

Forum Fontisiccense Urbis Campi Stellae

Exploratores pueri duo non pares videntur:
      princeps it ante posteaque agaso
    uterque felix: quam miser non particeps
      talibus historiis!

The Praza de Fonseca in Santiago de Compostela

The two boy scouts are obviously not equals;
the leader goes before and the lackey behind,
both of them happy; how wretched is he
who has no part in such stories!

Piscina Molaris Sturmonasterii Oppidi Novi

Cur modo nunc caeli quod habebitur omen haud aperti?
    Piscina forte visitur molaris:
  apparet improvisus unicus puer,
    aurum animans et ebur.

Tempus adest ut aquas temptet puer, intret aequor (euge!)
    mihi nefastum. Nonne oportet utar
  occasione? Me doces inutile:
    discere serus ero.

The Millpond at Sturminster Newton

Why just now, an event to be deemed an omen from an overcast
heaven? By chance a visit is made to a millpond;
alone and unforeseen a boy appears,
living gold and ivory.

It is time for the boy to test the waters, to enter – bravo! –
an expanse unlawful for me. Am I not supposed to make use
of opportunity? What you teach me is useless;
I shall be late in learning.

Laophorum prope Carteiam Provinciae Onobensis

Laophoro nimbus tibi ceditur aurei coloris.
      Sanctusne es? An peccator? An sodalis
   sodalium haud insignium ordinarius?
      Sive vocare putas

aethera sive negas attingere te deos sacrumque,
      iam rebus icon est creata tritis:
   erit necesse notiones caelitum
      insidiis saliant.

A Bus near Cartaya in the Province of Huelva

The bus provides you with a golden-coloured nimbus.
Are you a saint? Or a sinner? Or an ordinary companion
of unremarkable companions? Whether you think
you are called by ethereal regions

or deny that the gods and the holy can affect you,
everyday circumstances have made an icon;
it will be inevitable that ideas of heavenly beings
leap out from ambush.

Villa Millesiana prope Holmiam

Conficere hoc velit ars neque conficit, haud facit propinquum:
    coepisse cordis excitationem
  visis in ipsis rebus hic exponitur,
    nil statuisse oculum.

Exprimitur subito sapientia detegi vetanda:
    hic est, silete: panditur, tacete:
  natura demonstranda naturae fuit:
    iam sophe quid loqueris?

Millesgården near Stockholm

Art would like to create this but cannot, it cannot make anything
similar; here we find made clear that the arousal of the heart
has had its beginning just in the things seen, that this has not been
for the eye to decide.

Suddenly a wisdom is expressed which it ought to be forbidden
to uncover; here it is, be silent; it is laid open, do not speak;
the being of being was to be demonstrated;
what do you say now, O sage?

Prope Vestibulum Deversorii Londiniensis

Omnis inest virtus quae praebita poscitur poëtis:
    pulchrum esse, cautum, serium atque honestum.
  Quo neglegentis te dei iussu licet
    interea videam?

Credere me possim factum fore protinus vaporem,
    evaniturum lumine absoluto:
  miraculorum est me tuorum vivere
    te simul incolumem.

Near the Entrance-Hall of a London Hotel

Within you is every virtue that poets ask to be shown:
beauty, prudence, seriousness and honour.
By what order of a neglectful god am I meanwhile
allowed to see you?

I could believe I would forthwith have been turned to vapour,
vanish away in absolute light; the fact that I live
unharmed simultaneously with you is an example
of your wonders.

Stabulum Ovium Vici cui Nomen Menenses Camporum

Est caris calor: est ops mutua mos domesticorum.
        Servanda quae sunt his magis? Sodales,
    amore iuncti, proximi per sanguinem
            perpetuum foculum

semper alunt lignis sine quo fame destruantur omnes,
        frigore, siccitate. Non ut agni
    gens nostra pascens immolanda ducitur.
            Vivat amicitia!

A Sheep-Stall in the Village of Meneses de Campos

There is warmth for dear ones; mutual assistance is the custom
of the family. What things are more worth preserving
than these? Comrades, those joined by love,
those closest in blood

feed logs to an unfailing brazier without which all would be
destroyed by hunger, cold, drought. Our shepherding race
is not led to sacrifice as lambs are led.
Long live friendship!

37

Mater mea Portlandiae

Proletaria eo regalior ac laboriosa
      plerumque, quae lichenis hic decori
  paulisper auro suscipis gratum thronum
      vespere pacifero,

cor tibi, corde velut muliebribus ante te coactae
      parentibus, firmum ac fide potitum
  saxa aemulatur ista circum te quibus
      efficitur solium.

Materiem matrum primordia contulere rerum:
      absente mundi matre quid fuisset?
  Nam mater est aeterna rupes insulae
      quam coluere viri.

My Mother on Portland

You who are proletarian and all the more regal for that,
who though usually hardworking here for a moment
of a peaceful evening take to yourself a pleasant throne
among the gold of eye-cheering lichen:

as if you at heart had been gathered up by female kinfolk
before you, the heart within you, firm and rewarded
with trust, rivals the rocks around you from which
your lofty seat is formed.

The very beginnings of the universe brought together
the stuff mothers are made of; what would there have been
of the world without the mother? For the mother is the eternal stone
of the island men have cultivated.

Parentes mei Neptesque eorum
Adulescentulae

Praeterit usque aetas, aequos facit, aequilibrium aufert,
      quocumque iunctos promovet pedestres
  metasque tendit nesciis quales. Diem
      degimus ambiguum.

My Parents and their Granddaughters
as Young Teenagers

Our lifetime passes continually by, making equals of us, depriving us
of balance, moving us forward on foot together in whatever direction
and holding out goals the nature of which is unknown to us.
It is an ambiguous day we are spending.

Parentes mei Neptesque eorum Puellulae

Possumus interdum dimittere vel fugare curas,
  sed cuncta oblectamenta finientur
  valentque degravare serum saeculum
    gaudia nata hodie.

My Parents and their Granddaughters as Little Girls

At times we are able to put aside or chase away
our cares, but all pleasures will be terminated
and joys born today have power to weigh down
upon a later age.

Parentes mei Stantes praeter Rosas

Vos in luce proba bene vivere nec latere vidi
    scioque claras vos rosas amasse.
  Si terga vobis florum in hos dulcissimos
      vertere iam libuit,

cur tabulas vultis vos ducere codicesve planos?
    Nonne hinc iter notum sit atque certum?
  Viam fidelem rete rugarum monet
    alterius facie.

My Parents Standing beyond Roses

I have seen you in honourable light living well and not
hiding away, and I know you to have loved bright roses.
If you have chosen now to turn your backs on these
most sweet of flowers,

why want maps or open-flat books to guide you?
Surely the journey from here is familiar and certain?
The dependable way is shown by the net of wrinkles
in the other's face.

His Mother is a Fire

His mother is a fire
held in a sea of stone.
Eternities of ire
are what the nerve had known
till he was thrown, half-done,
into the cooling air
where only a distant sun
reminded him of there
and where he grew to be
what mocks at shapes of flame,
a flickering, glittering tree,
a person and a name,
blessing the rain that fell
to solace him for hell.

He sometimes thinks of hell.
The reason? He has burned.
The future cannot tell
such pain as he has learned.
Now in his heaven, earth,
he shudders: hell was that.
Happiness succeeds birth
and is a thermostat.
The fears that others nursed,
and hopes, he knows for vain.
He has been through the worst.
There is no more to gain
than earth's ultimate height
and refreshment and light.

De Quodam Nervo

Illius mater nihil est nisi ignis
    quem sumpsit mare saxeum tenetque.
        Sempiterna enim Nervum ira cremabat
           alvo quoad depulsus aëra hausit
semicoctus nare refrigerantem.
    Solo sole procul memor caloris
        factus est quod inridet sibi formam
           moresque flammae, scilicet coruscans
clara recta arbor tremula atque acuta.
    Notus nomine nobili notatur
        Nervus ac libens imbri benedicit,
           solacio terroris inferorum.

Inferos Nervus reputat subinde.
    Quanam re? Quod in inferis flagravit.
        Nescient futura agnoscere tantum
           quantum ille quondam passus est dolorem.
Facta terra est caelum animo trementi,
    quin vix cepit abesse quo peribat:
        gaudium ante partum excluserat aestus,
           thermostatum aurae sivit esse laetum.
Spem metusque altos aliis inanes
    novit, nam tulit ultimum periclum
        sospes: aethera integrum atque lucentem
           tangit: quid optet praeter hunc petendum?

Venus and Vulcan, warm
either in either's way,
drank of their teacup storm,
harvested sunshine hay.
Violent, vital, vain,
neither cared in the least
what tossed into the wain,
what was left to the beast.
Wretched conjunctio
of juices on the stone,
what would, what could they know
of embryo flesh and bone
and mind and spirit too
and hope of something new?

His fine perviousness!
See what he has been made.
A plume and Icarus,
a fern and a whole glade;
what sways in every wind,
at every warmth unrolls,
lightly-moved, tender-skinned,
and thinks in terms of souls;
whom yet a knot of threads
fastening to the ground
sufficiently embeds
in what the world goes round;
enough root and no more
in generation's floor.

Vana potabant Venus et vigente
   Vulcanus violentia procellae
      guttulam: calore aestatis apricum
         foenum benignis casibus metabant:
neuter omnino fatuus quot essent
   plaustro fragmina, quot feris darentur
      scire vellet. O duram sine lecto
         coniunctionem vilium liquorum!
Nulla dis cura incipientis ossis
   est carnisve adytis recentis ovi.
      Indoles quid est dis ingeniosa
         valebimusve quod novum patrare?

Perviae textu tenuesque netu
   factus quae sit imagines videte:
      pluma et Icarus, fissae filicis frons
         nemusque totum: qui movetur aura
quaque: quem quivis tepor explicabit:
   qui praefert animas modis decoris:
      qui cutem est tener, vibrans agilisque:
         quem nodus autem staminum ligavit
in solum firme satis, inque amorem
   molem qui ciet et cietur ipse:
      Nervus ut solo, Nervo satis haeret
         (nec plus) humus, fons omnium ac sepulcrum.

To a Clarinettist

My love, if I were blind,
then would you take my part;
with pity in your mind
and deep thoughts in your heart
you'd bend to let me touch
your sweet and darkened face:
you will not grant so much
intimacy and grace
to an unbroken reed.
Must I be cut and shaped
to be worthy your kiss?
See how my soul is scraped
by sorrow's knife! I bleed!
But you'll not bend for this.

Time

These fragile, twisted leaves
like ashes, these contain
a virtue which their thieves
esteem; in them remain
all the essential oils
life paid them to uplay;
what robbers pick for spoils
the pious choose for prey;
savour the scent of time,
its distinct concentrate!
Take in what glistening rime,
rain-love and hailstone-hate
and feral feet and fun
and great Iamb have done.

Ad Tibicinem

Mel meum, si caecus amicus essem
    tunc ferres mihi opem: libente clemens
        mente cogitansque abscondita venis
            deflectereris ut tuam tenebris
tangerem dulcem faciem. Negabis
    non fracto calamove arundinive
        gratiam intimam: caedine opus esset
            fortasse formarique iam priore
sorte quassato mihi ut ore dignus
    mellito fierem? Vide cruentum
        cor doloris hic rasum mihi cultro!
            Videns tamen non flecteris videnti.

Tempus

Hae pares frondes cineri retortae
    virtutem fragiles bene aestimatam
        furibus tenent: illic oleorum
            potentium est vis empta tota vitae
sumptibus, praeda optima partienda
    pravis aut precibus piis petenda.
        Temporis thymi gustate sapores,
            succos, medullas, musta torcularis:
noscite et quod splendida in his pruina,
    imber carus et haud amata grando
        et pedes ferarum et gaudia iambi
            fecere et illud "sum", salubre summum.

Some Are Like Frogs

Some are like frogs and live
now in, now by their pond;
but me the love-blue O
repulses, and the sieve
on which the foolish fond
fain travel weighs my woe.
Half love, the soft sands give
under my finnish feet.
I climb on to a frond
and bid the dry wind blow.
There is no word to greet
me, and my heart is dry:
dry like the peace-blue sky,
tandemity's clear eye.

On Stony Ground I Fell

On stony ground I fell,
but am nearly all stone.
Out of a single cell
a slender thread had grown
and fretted, frayed and burst
this carapace. And I,
condemned with what I cursed,
here with the liars lie,
laid down indeed, and must
hide here with other hard
in space's breaker's yard:
for softness dries to dust
soon lost in breath's last gust:
my shell is shown a shard.

Aequa cum Ranis

Aequa cum ranis coluit lacunam
  gens ripamque, sed O nota hunc poëtam
    blanda caerula absterret: gravat illud
      in quo libenter victimae vehuntur
cribrum Amoris maestitiam paventi.
  Squamosis pedibus meis harena
    mollis haud Amoris cesserit expers
      scandamque in herbam, flare postulabo
spiritum siccum, neque vox salutem
  ullam dicet: erit meum cor aeque
    siccum, erit polo pax caerula sicca:
      "tandem" sonabit lumen arefactum.

Scrupeam in Terram

Scrupeam in terram cecidi, tamen me
  saxum paene merum esse confitebor.
    Quem vides fricatum, tritum et abruptum
      ab involucris creveram modo uno
fibra de grano tenuis: sed inde
condemnatus ego ut mihi exsecrati,
    mentientium mendis maculatus,
      demotus inter asperos iacere,
cosmicis scrutis proprius latere
  cogor. Namque fit omne molle siccus
    pulvus halitu mox mortis abactus.
      Quod crustam habebam testa iam videtur.

Vesta's Red Fang-Rimmed Lap

Vesta's red fang-rimmed lap
turns Venus' foam to steam:
the escape, the valve, the vent,
the orifice, the gap
which with a panic scream
in the white wall is rent
casts bathed in ichor forth
the salamander babe;
who finds a fiery pap
but is denied and sent
ignorant of life's North,
wanting an astrolabe
into the cold night dream
and joys of things that seem.

Lazarus

Lazarus in the tomb
waiting to be reborn
cries perhaps to his God:
"Who laid me in this womb,
forsaken and forlorn?
Beyond this stone Who trod?
Came He but to perfume
carrion and to mourn?
Or was I on His rod
spun, and stretched on His loom?
Am I His robe untorn?
Did the rogues push and prod
me or Him in their scorn?
And: when I cry – to Whom?"

Vesta Dentato Gremio

Vesta dentato gremio rubente
    spumam albam Veneris facit vaporem:
        dein foramen in muro sine labe
            ruptum pavoris eiulatione,
exitum, spiramen, hiatus, antrum,
    ichore edit inunctam et uber ardens
        parvulam statim nactam salamandram:
            quae mox inexpleta exsul avolabit
nesciens sidus Boreale vitae,
    astrorum sophia carens et armis,
        somnium in gelatum vecta tenebris
            gaudensque rebus tantum adulterinis.

Lazarus

Lazarus nunc opperiens sepulcro
    dum bis nascitur invocat Supremum
        territus: "Quis hac alvo posuit me
            sic derelictum perditumque? Quisnam
praeter hunc gressus lapidem est? Et illum
    advenisse putem modo ut putrescens
        suffiat cadaver conlacrimetque?
            Netumne virga me putem Magistri,
tentum et in tela Domini Creantis,
    non scissam tunicam? Meum scelestam
        turmam an illius corpus stimulasse?
            Quandoque clamo, quem volo vocari?"

THE BOX OF BALM

HORACE
People at parties are asking why a strange scent
pervades the piece dedicated to Virgil,
"Iam veris comites", following number eleven
in my recent book of poems.

LIGURINUS
The source of their disquiet's unclear to any of those
who usually enjoy the charm of poetry;
for only I, young Ligurinus, a boy wiser than his age,
am able to perceive it.

HORACE
I knew that you, Ligurinus, had been boldly boasting
you understood it all; but to tell the truth
I was not bothered by that sort of thing;
you can reveal the secrets.

LIGURINUS
Then let me define the main question put by a connoisseur
who for the first time comes across the poem.
You bring in, rather cruelly, the awful story of Procne –
in what way is that appropriate to the poem?

HORACE
The treacherous queen who took revenge on her husband
by cooking their son for food will rightly be detested;
however the woman's story is here of little importance,
what the bird does of the greatest.

Onyx Nardi

HORATIUS
Cur insuetus odor Vergilio tegat
    opus dicatum quaeritur conviviis:
"Iam veris comites", undecimum quod sequitur libro
        meo recenti carminum.

LIGURINUS
Nullis perspicuum est unde sit inquies
    frui lepore versuum solentibus:
solus namque potis percipere hoc sum Ligurinulus
        puer diebus doctior.

HORATIUS
Te scivi, Ligurine, omnia cognita
    habere verbis gloriatum audacibus: 10
at sane mihi non exhibuit tale molestiam:
        licet recludere abdita.

LIGURINUS
Ergo praecipuam iudicis inscii
    poëma nacti quaestionem finiam:
Procnes historiam terribilem saevius implicas:
        ad ista qua re pertinet?

HORATIUS
Regina ulta virum perfida filio
    cibo coquendo rite detestata erit:
momenti tamen hic exigui fabula feminae,
        volucris actus maximi.   20

LIGURINUS

The bird builds its home on walls in spring,
but another meaning appears in the verses,
for to Virgil, a poet long dead, nest-building time
is of little relevance.

The woman had killed her own womb's son; when you said
farewell to your much loved comrade who had succumbed
to death, was not a certain amount of guilt stowed away
in the depths of your heart?

You take upon yourself the guilt for his death contending,
typically for you, that the verb "to kill" can imply
"to afflict with something no-one is able to bear";
you had laid a burden upon your friend.

Maecenas learnt from your poems an abundance of questioning
could kill. You think your best friend died
from the surfeit of pride in your mind; he was a man
no longer young, stricken with worry,

convinced that fortune would always remain at a distance
from Maro, himself, while fighting his way across the breadth
of the Aeneid, toiling for gorgeous language yet doubtful
of the outcome achieving renown.

You on the other hand, striking the stars with the crown
of your head, a singer of songs more lasting than bronze,
a swan of Melpomene feathered on fingers and shoulders
(you delight in a seriously meant jest)

were presenting the look of a bard by Apollo's favour
more worthy of fame than others; whether you liked
to credit yourself with supremacy at your Sabine
retreat I do not know.

LIGURINUS
Ales vere domum moenibus instruit,
  sed altera exstat versibus sententia:
refert tempus enim nidificum Vergilii parum
  diu poëtae mortui.

Interfecerat haec natum uteri sui:
  tuum sodalem morte dilectissimum
affanti domitum nonne tibi culpa aliquanta erat
  retenta corde in intimo?

In te culpam obitus suscipis arguens
  tenere verbum "occidere" hunc sensum tuum,   30
"re quam nullus homo ferre potest afficere ardua":
  onus sodali ieceras.

Maecenas didicit carminibus tuis
  rogationum copias occidere.
Credis tu nimia quae tibi erat mente superbia
  amicum obivisse optimum,

qui non iam iuvenis, sollicitus, ratus
  Marone semper stare fortunam procul,
pugnabat dubius magniloquo nobilis exitus
  labore trans Aeneida.   40

Tu contra feriens vertice sidera,
  perenniorum cantor aere carminum,
plumatus digitos atque umeros Melpomenes olor
  (ioco iuvaris serio)

praebebas speciem vatis Apolline
  favente fama dignioris ceteris:
num gratum fuerit noscere te non superabilem
  apud Sabinos nescio.

Pointed out by passers-by as the Latin lyre's wholly
accomplished master, roaming around and plucking
flowers, you arrange a wealth of poetical rhythms
on the Muses' turf;

he like a tiller of the field, not taking the ample
rest he deserves, furrows with inherited ploughshare
straight, unbroken, unvarying, dutiful hexameters,
an epic, georgics, eclogues.

The obvious difference between your rôles meant you and he
have not been regarded as rivals by partial factions.
Your protection and glory, that man descended from kings,
gave both of you equal support.

Only Virgil was of another mind; his increased ill-feeling
towards you gnawed more grievously at his bowels
just when you to the same degree were being less pained
by envy's tooth.

Finally he died. However you with your flourishing talent
were opportunely brought by the Centenary Song
to the attention of the people, and by your unjust sense of guilt
to the remorse which guilt aroused.

HORACE
I have been listening with glowing interest. How many
salt tears there flowed before in my wretchedness
I wrote the poem longing, alas, to give you,
Virgil, a friend's embrace!

LIGURINUS
You address your Virgil with a supplication: for his cup
to be filled he should quickly bring a little box of balm –
a suitable gift from a guest at a feast but also
appropriate to the tomb.

Monstratus digito praetereuntium
    lyrae Latinae perpolitus arbiter   50
tu circumvagus ac florilegus caespite musico
    opes modorum conlocas:

ille ut cultor agri vomere patrio
    arat sine amplo quod meretur otio
rectos continuos haud varios hexametros pios,
    epos, georgica, eclogas.

Non estis cupidis partibus aemuli
    patente ducti munerum discrimine.
Aeque vos atavis praesidium regibus editum
    fovebat et decus tuum.   60

Soli Vergilio mens erat altera:
    adauctus illi livor erga te simul
rodebat gravius viscera dum dente pari gradu
    minus dolebas invido.

Tandem mortuus est. Te tamen attulit
    vigente Saeculare Carmen indole
mature publicam ad notitiam, culpaque ad excitam
    iniqua paenitentiam.

HORATIUS
Audivi studio non sine fervido.
    Quot ante manavere salsae lacrimae   70
quam scripsi misere carmen avens heu tibi, Vergili,
    sodalis amplexum dare!

LIGURINUS
Supplex adloqueris Vergilium tuum:
    ut impleatur poculum velox ferat
nardi parvum onychem, donum epulis hospitis utile
    sed et sepulcri proprium.

Why should your friend supply balm from the regions
of the Styx, he whom you named in prophetic lines, when
a fragile bark had sailed away, half of your own soul?
Might you now have chosen to die?

I do not think the two of you can again by other paths
come to one place, whatever it be, nor were it fitting
to restore to its original state your single complete
soul outside the underworld;

for Diana does not return the king's son from infernal
darkness to the living, nor, eloquent one, does the strength
of Theseus succeed in sundering the chains of Lethe
for Pirithous' sake.

Across your burning forehead longing and imagined
fault moisten you with an evil sweat; only balm,
the dense fat of a soon to be hollow cadaver,
soothes and cools.

It is not strange there should be a strange scent in the air,
of green grass together with the unguent of the tombs.
With well-chosen words you beautify a theme hardly
in harmony with itself; heart disagrees with palate.

    HORACE
What may be false, what true Horace does not disclose,
nor whether he himself has the whole matter in his grasp.
Sometimes I know for certain less than I feel diffusely; when you read,
find enjoyment in whatever way you can.

Cur nardum socius de Styge commodet,
   vocatus a te versibus praenuntiis
provecta fragili nave animae dimidium tuae?
      Morine nunc optaveris?   80

Vos nullis aliter posse viis puto
   venire in unum denuo quemvis locum,
nec vestram deceat solam animam ad principium integram
      reducere extra Tartara:

infernis neque enim de tenebris refert
   Diana regis filium viventibus,
nec Lethaea valent Pirithoo vincula abrumpere,
      diserte, vires Theseos.

Te desiderium fictaque noxia
   malo rigant sudore per frontem igneam: 90
tantum nardus, adeps mox vacui crassa cadaveris,
      remulcet ac refrigerat.

Haud mire sit odor mirus in aëre
   virentis herbae cum sepulcrorum unguine.
Facundus decoras propositum vix sibi congruens:
      cor a palato dissidet.

HORATIUS
Quae sint falsa tacet, vera etiam tacet
   Horatius numve ipse totum ceperit.
Interdum sapio certa minus quam vaga sentio:
      legens oblectare ut queas.   100

The Weasel: or rather, Telamus

What was the name Mustela, Weasel,   intended to say? "We lie
hidden." Telamus used to be   a river; now he shines
as a boy in bronze. Do not lie hidden,   weasel; the boy has to reach
and get to know you; Telamus is   the lord of his own weasel,
and you'll not be able to hide yourself   for long, shut in a hollow
under rugged stones; you'll not put up   with enclosure. Apollo used
to tint the river with scattered silver;   now he throws his light
on the river-like statue of a boy;   the coating of oxidization
spreads out like a reflection of   the circle above, and the dark
bronze spreads out like what lies deep   down among the waters.
Telamus, now that you have followed   the first tracks of the weasel,
grasp her soft neck tenderly   with an eager hand.

Good reader, how would you like me to introduce
the iambics? This you consider too prosaic:
"Have a look at Otto Strandman's notable bronze,
the weasel and boy, placed in Kungsholmen Square;
Stockholm has nothing to show more worthy of
a worthy poet." You see, one's ears feel numbed
and bored by a presentation such as that.
May minds receive enjoyment from the verses.

The Creator took flesh; this is thought most wonderful,
but what more certain sign of God could there be?
Though unchangeable He outdid Himself so that we,
faithless human beings, might be changed.

We have heard of journeys of more exalted beings
to our humble soil. Ours is not only the Hebrew heritage
but also that left us by Greeks, adorers of deities
that made themselves into people, birds and beasts.

MUSTELA VEL POTIUS TELAMUS

Dicere quid voluit nomen Mustela? "Latemus."
    Telamus amnis erat: nunc puer aere nitet.
Ne lateas mustela: puer te noscat adeptus:
    mustelae propriae Telamus est dominus,
nec poteris cavea saeptam saxis sub iniquis
    te celare diu: non patiere modum.
Argento sparso fluvium tingebat Apollo:
    flumineam lustrat nunc statuam pueri:
panditur aerugo superi velut orbis imago
    aesque atrum quae sunt funditus inter aquas.
Telame mustelae vestigia prima secutus
    collum instante tener lene prehende manu.

Quomodo vis introducam bone lector iambos?
    Nimis pedestre iudicas
"Ottonis Ripensis opus spectabile aënum
    Regalis Insulae Foro
mustelam puerumque vide: nihil Holmia praebet
    digno poëta dignius."
Talis enim taedet stupefactas lemmatis aures.
    Mentes fruantur versibus.

Carnem Creator sumpsit: hoc mirissimum
pensatur, at num certius signum Dei
fieri potuerit? Semet immutabilis
superavit ut mutemur homines perfidi.

Excelsiorum iter ad solum humile agnovimus.
Non tantum Hebraea est nostra sed et hereditas
legata Graecis, qui coluerant numina
viros mulieres facta aves ac bestias.

If such deities are imagined in muddled myths
to have changed their shapes for disgraceful practices' sake,
so much more proper for God to outdo Himself
to bring our own people news of healthful things.

The created takes song and flies into the sky
like a lark; he ascends where the Lord descended; carried
through upper air by the power of an eagle he enters
into Ganymede's noble servitude.

Now let the body of Telamus be considered.
Backwards behind him he stretches his right leg;
one who believes in his own position will stand
on upright legs; here Telamus bows submissive.

Almost as showing respect to a higher authority
he places his left knee on the rough rock, the earth
rising thus up to Telamus so that his knees
may be stable before a precarious destiny.

One arm thrusts down what has been, the other invites
the future into the present while protecting
an innocent breast – or is it about to attack
the lissom animal with an agile right hand?

The boy's waist (O golden mean!) is slender in form,
so that the upper body may move more smoothly
in the strenuous deftnesses of the wrestling school
and dancing in a company of youths.

Is not Telamus seen here bowing most charmingly
his sweet head in a graceful pose, receiving
the office of cupbearer from the supreme father
of the family of celestial beings, Jupiter?

Si tale se mutasse numen fingitur
ut turpia ageret fabulis inconditis,
superavit aptius unicus sese Deus
res ut salubres nuntiet nostratibus.

Carmen creatus sumit et volat in polum
simulans alaudam: scandit ubi descenderat
Dominus: per aethera vectus aquilae viribus
Ganymedis intrat servitutem nobilem.

Consideretur corpus autem Telami.
Post se retrorsum porrigit crus dexterum:
stet crure recto qui potens fidet sibi:
proclinat obsequiosus hic se Telamus.

Paene quasi qui veneretur imperium altius
genu sinistrum conlocat saxo rudi,
terra sublata sic ad ipsum Telamum
ut genua sedeant ante fata precaria.

Quod iam fuit detrudit utrum bracchium,
utrum futura invitat in praesentia
insonsque pectus protegit, nisi mox dabit
subitum ictum in animal mobile agili dextera.

Pueri media pars (aurea o mediocritas!)
formae gracilis est ut superior mollius
moveatur artibus in palaestra strenuis
saltationeque cum maribus aliis choro.

Nonne hic videtur Telamus lepidissime
gestu decoro suave submittens caput,
munus recipiens proferendi poculi
de Iove supremo patre familiae caelitum?

He looks down as if enticed hither by something glistening;
so young Hylas was led astray by evil nymphs,
he who as prince had weakened the vigorous, mighty
strength of the hero Argonaut Hercules.

He looks down as if seeking proof in some weighty matter;
so Narcissus looked down at his own appearance;
who is more beautiful than Telamus or
more fitted to be reborn as a charming flower?

He looks down as if quietly having thought of a joke;
thus did Hyacinthus the pupil mock the posture
from which the hapless discus-thrower, playmate,
lover, beloved destroyer, released destruction.

Hyacinthus changed second into a flower of spring,
dead Adonis, become a scarlet anemone, third,
and the race we belong to is a sweet-scented garden,
but Telamus is to be favoured beyond all others.

The river flowed down; he flows upwards, replacing with lightness
what heaviness his body possessed, a flower
of fluidness; rightly do Britons write with identical
letters the words for "blossom" and "he who flows"!

In the day of the prophets, in the dark ages and
the renascent and also recently, is not every
boy among the saints considered handsome
and every holy virgin proclaimed to be fair?

So children pleasing to God are said to have been
as outstanding in their looks as in their spirits.
Why? Because only with respect to the beauty
of bodies could we believe God to be even more beautiful.

Despicit ut huc pellectus aliquo fulgido:
sic iuvenis Hylas abductus est nymphis malis
qui robur acre et grande debilitaverat
herois Herculis Argonautae regulus.

Despicit ut indicium appetens causa gravi:
Narcissus ita despexit in faciem suam:
quis Telamo sit pulchrior vel idoneus
magis ut venustus cras renasci flosculus?

Despicit ut animo placidus intuitus iocum:
Hyacinthus ita discipulus inrisit statum
quo discobolus infaustus obiecit necem
conlusor et amans atque amatus perditor.

Hyacinthus alter vernus est flos redditus,
tertius Adonis rubra anemone mortuus,
hortusque odorum dulcium gens quae sumus:
at diligendus praeter alios Telamus.

Fluxit deorsum flumen: hic sursum fluit
levitate supplens grave quod habuit corpore,
flos fluiditatis: rite iisdem litteris
voces Britanni "fluctor" et "flos" exarant!

Nonne in prophetarum die, tam saeculis
caliginosis quam renatis ac recens
formosus omnis habetur in sanctis puer
omnisque virgo sancta pulchra edicitur?

Narrantur ergo liberi grati Deo
specie similiter praestitisse ac spiritu.
Qua re? Quod una pulchritudine corporum
Deum potuimus pulchriorem credere.

Is heaven reserved for such as these alone?
In the same way it makes sense that when we cast
our eyes on earth's fairest offspring and are lifted
beyond the clouds we too are allowed into heaven.

Meanwhile aware in passing of the ambusher
the little beast raises her head and all wide awake
stiffens, afraid of assault by slender hands
and ignorant of what imminent struggle may bring.

We have few Telamuses among mankind,
but each has plenty in his soul of the weasel,
desirous, fearful, uncertain of her end
or of the hand that strokes with subverting love.

Beauty of the Telamus who is forgetful
of the past, mindful of things to come, adroit
at games, not hidden from light, reach also me;
overturn and upraise me, touch me, empty and fill me!

Num talibus modo sit reservatus polus?
Haud aliter intellegitur admitti polo
nos qui videntes filios pulcherrimos
telluris extollemur ultra nubila.

Hoc tempore insidiantis obiter conscia
bestiola caput erexit et riguit vigil,
manuum tenuium timida ne dent impetum,
ignara quid certamen afferat imminens.

Paucos in hominum prole habemus Telamos,
sed multam in anima quisque mustelam tenet
quae cupida pavida incertaque est finis sui
vel amore subvertente palpantis manus.

Adipiscere et me, pulchritudo Telami,
praeteritum obliti, providi venientium,
ludis periti, lumini non conditi:
subverte et erige, tange, fac inanem et reple!

THRICE YEARNING VOICE
(from the margins of the Gospels)

A Boy

Remit, I pray, the thousand great debts which I cannot
pay back and which I will never be able to discharge;
but accept nonetheless the few poor gifts I bear;
is it a worthless bag that holds five barley loaves

prepared over the fire by my mother's hand – the offspring
has received everything from its parents – and two fishes
seized in my father's net? And can any of this be
a blessing to the multitude? I surrender nothing

to the crowd, the food is handed to you alone: may it be drawn
into realms above that are worthy of you. Like a man
leaving on a journey you have given your servant with regard
to his strengths living talents to be augmented in value,

I know not how great or of what sort. Money acquires profit
by the art of the money-lender; increase, I beg, by your art
what has been entrusted to your servant, for what
can we bring before you unless it be from what is yours?

To whom, if not to you, Christ, should we make over our talents?
It is your image the coin here boasts! I hand myself over to you,
bread and fish to you who created me: be yourself the maker
of something more from my food and my innate potential.

Accept and distribute the loaves, oh share out the fishes,
but restore the crumbs that are not to be consumed
of the produce given out, lest anything be lost, or lest I be left
behind and lost; O Christ, keep me safe, thriving and whole.

Vox Ter Cupida

Loquuntur e marginibus Evangeliorum puer, adulescens, iuvenis

Puer

Reddere quae nequeo, potero quae solvere nunquam
    rogo remitte mille magna debita:
at quae pauca fero tamen accipe paupera dona:
    inopsne saccus hordeaceos habet

quinque manu matris panes super igne paratos
    (recepit omne partus a parentibus)
atque duos pisces correptos rete paterno?
    Et ecquid inde multitudinem beet?

Nil turbae dedo, tibi soli traditur esca:
    trahatur in superna digna te loca.
Sicut homo peregre proficiscens viva ministro
    talenta, quanta nesciove qualia,

respiciens proprias vires augenda dedisti.
    Pecunia arte nummularii lucrum
obtinet: arte tua, precor, auge credita servo:
    quid afferamus ante te nisi ex tuo?

Cui nisi Christe tibi tradamus nostra talenta?
    Tuam nomisma iactat hic imaginem.
Me trado tibi, me panem piscemque creanti:
    fac ipse maius escam et indolem meam.

Distribue acceptos panes, o divide pisces,
    sed haud edenda frusta frugis editae
restituas ne quid pereat pereamve relictus:
    tuere Christe me virentem et integrum.

A Youth

Unseasoned by years I had not grown up;
having followed a just man across my formerly
customary limits I became forthwith fearful
of peril from unknown things to come.

As if to catch a thief a gang of villains
came in the night with swords to seize
one who had often spoken by day
to the craving people in the temple in Jerusalem.

Stricken with fright every disciple
deserted his master; I, just as alarmed
as the throng, happened to run
towards one of the villains.

The enemy stretched out his supple arm
and grasped the edge of my linen garment in his hand.
I struggled backwards in order to slip away
and was suddenly a naked figure.

Thus I fled then disoriented on trembling legs
through the narrow streets. With my mind in tumult
I was guiltily aware that mysteries had been defiled
by this ridiculous, unseemly turn of events.

Do an open temperament, dawn in one's countenance,
pleasing manners carry any weight?
Is worthy the epithet sensible folk
in every era give slender youth?

Certainly I deem unworthy what I was turning over
then in my brain, worried at having fled in disgrace,
for to whom could it matter that I went in darkness
without the clothing of modesty?

Adulescens

Insulsus annis non adoleveram:
iustum secutus trans solitos prius
    fines ab ignotis futuris
        protinus extimui periclum.

Tamquam ad latronem cum gladiis globus
venit malorum nocte prehendere
    vulgo requirenti locutum
        saepe die Solymis in aede.

Plaga pavoris discipulus citus
omnis magistrum deseruit suum:
    cum mole consternatus aeque
        forte malo propius cucurri.

Porrexit hostis mobile bracchium,
percepit oram sindonis in manu,
    retro sublapsurus tetendi,
        nuda fui subito figura:

dein crure fugi sic tremulo vagus
vicos per artos: mente tumultuans
    arcana sons polluta sensi
        ridicula vice et indecora.

Pondusne portant ingenium patens,
aurora vultu, moris amoenitas,
    dignamve prudentes per aeva
        cuncta vocant gracilem iuventam?

Quae nempe turpi sollicitus fuga
volvi cerebro digna parum reor,
    nam cuius intersit tenebris
        me sine veste pudoris isse?

Though I am always at any moment an examplar
of the Lord God's image, having emerged
from invisibility with my own identity,
the soul's rights being undeniable –

until I gain a man's status, as who do I truly exist,
being still all too insignificant? What rôle,
exempt from bloodshed as lately from suckling,
belongs to the orphan of the present moment?

Unseen guardian, ask neither patience nor false
colours of me; purely as I am let me be viewed,
rushing through eternal stars and entering
a refuge plain to every eye.

A Young Man

Women, nothing has made me so happy as this matter.
Believe one who tells the truth; listen and be glad in your hearts.
Do not be afraid of anything, for he whom you seek,
Christ Jesus, is elsewhere; he has risen here from the dead;

inspect the place where his body was buried; is it not
empty enough? But pass on the message he sends
to his shattered fosterlings and Peter their leader: soon
his native Galilee will bring the holy company back together;

there the master will be seen after his crucifixion;
the faithful band should make haste by the northern
road. Go then; but if you will delay, learn what sort
of tree there is in this funereal garden,

as it were a second, a tree of death just as in the beginning
there was a tree of knowledge. With the change of seasons
its shoots become almost black. It is named the yew
and said when eaten to be fatal both to beasts

Exemplar etsi semper imaginis
quavis in hora sum Domini Dei,
 qui noscor ex caligine ortus,
  iure animae minime negando,

donec virilem promerear statum
vere quis exsto parvus adhuc nimis,
 persona quae praesentis orbi
  sanguinis ut modo lactis expers?

Invise custos, ne patientiam
neu posce fucum: conspiciar merus
 aeterna festinans per astra et
  ingrediens manifestum asylum.

Iuvenis

Iuvit nihil me sicut haec res, feminae:
credite veridico: audite, gaudete in sinu!
 Nolite quid timere, nam quem quaeritis
Christus Iesus abest: surrexit hic a mortuis:

locum sepulti corporis scrutamini:
nonne satis vacuus? Quem mittit autem nuntium
 fractis alumnis tradite et Petro duci:
mox Galilaea domus coetum recomponet sacrum:

illic magister post crucem videbitur:
fida manus properet septentrionum tramite.
 Eatis ergo: si moremini tamen
discite qualis in hoc sit arbor horto funebri,

ceu mortis esset altera ut scientiae
arbor origine erat. Mutatione temporum
 virgae nigrescunt paene: taxus dicitur
nomine, dicitur et fatalis esa bestiis

and to the human governors of all creation. Let
the two-legged keep away! Let the herdsman be on his guard!
But the berry of the yew is sweet, and pretty also,
and likewise harmless if one spits out its hard stone.

He whom you were to anoint is not here. What of this?
As he himself has stated, he was the Anointed since the beginning
of the ages. Gloomy death no longer holds the bright dead one:
does the Lord's absence despite yourselves fill you with fear?

In your minds compare, as is fitting, his absence with this tree;
it looks sorrowful but in its darkness there is hope,
beautiful with the colour of the rose, honey-sweet and good.
Reject this foliage of mute grief, do not be harmed

by the stone of mourning while down your throats
its flesh slips rich in wonder. Would Christ
have disappeared neglecting his own? So long
as mortality and to live, to be born and God,

truth and to invent, woman and to be a man, at length
to grow old and erstwhile delightful youth are counted
as paradoxical, pleasing contradiction saves by love
a kind which only unyieldingness can destroy.

creationisque omnis humanis eris.
Abstineant bipedes! Cautus sit armentarius!
    Sed baca taxi dulcis est, venusta item
nec minus innocua durum spuenti nucleum.

    Unguendus ille vester hic non est. Quid hoc?
Unctus ut ipse tulit aevis ab inceptis erat.
    Non iam tenet mors atra clarum mortuum:
vosne replet Domini absentia invitas metu?

    Absentiam apte mente conferte arbori:
maesta videtur, at huic obscuritati spes inest
    rosae colore pulchra, mellita ac bona.
Reicite haec folia muti doloris, lugubri

    nolite laedi nucleo cuius simul
pulpa gulis satura mirationis defluat.
    Vanesceretne neglegens Christus suos?
Dum paradoxa valent mortalitas et vivere,

    nasci Deusque, veritas et fingere,
femina et esse virum, tandem senescere atque adhuc
    suavis iuventus, grata contradictio
servat amore genus solo rigore perditum.

In Djursholm

I used to hold the book's pages open to write –
oughtn't they now to be opened to be read?
In spring the truth shall be dealt with, I enter
spring to unlock it.

The waters of this channel are the image
of a bowl painted in a myriad of blues,
bringing the gullet a power of tasty morsels,
sweet, salt and sour.

Germania has given this water its name:
that blue youngsterdom of Horace, a monster
but handsome warring in the sixteenth epode –
be the colour due

to the woad of the fields or noted in the splendour
of eyes or put to the test in choiceness of clothing
as by the painter Gainsborough in his picture
of a boy –

has that youngsterdom for its one true home
this bay of the northern seas which I have
visited often, where I am sitting at this
very moment?

An azure colour often sends out a sign
that what we might want to eat should not be eaten;
heaven itself warns us of danger and so
does the flowing sea.

But so many things have been or are still forbidden;
may it not be time to defy long-standing
prohibitions? When am I to be king
if not now?

EXTEMPORALIA ANTE VER INCEPTUM

Diursolmiae

Paginas libri scripturus apertas
    quondam tenebam: nonne iam recludi
    debent legendae? Vere verum agetur,
        ver reserandum ineo.

Sunt aquae freti crateris imago
    turba colorum picta caerulorum:
    dulcem gulae salsamque mattearum
        vimque refert acidam.

His aquis dedit Germania nomen:
    Horatiine caerula illa pubes
    bellata belua atque bella epodo
        in sexto decimo,

seu color vitro debetur agresti
    seu luminum splendore noscitatur
    seu sicut a pictore Gensboroeo
        in tabula pueri

elegantia tentatur amictus,
    veram domum unam fluctibus Boreis
    habet sinus quem saepe visitavi,
        hic modo ubi sedeo?

Saepe caerulus signum color edit
    haud esculentorum cibariorum:
    caelo pericla praemonemur ipso
        atque liquente mari.

Tot tamen diu res sunt vetitae vel
    et nunc vetantur: nonne sit necesse
    contemnere interdicta longa? Quando
        rex nisi nunc fierem?

Shan't I take my fate upon myself? What
I'd written a quarter of a century before
not daring to believe I was taking down
another's dictation,

but thinking it all my own invention –
these words from the past I've disinterred
to read them as an older man, if possible
as an impartial judge.

It's good and quiet here. The unfolder of truth
desires the lecture hall to be silent, spring tells
the garden and the woods to be silent so that all
may grow anew.

It's good and quiet here. Determined to be established
is peace before spring, peace before truth. It is pleasant
to sit here in front of the book of an art still
unrevealed inside.

Many a diagram of the cross in the hues of crocus
and tulip is contained by the little book. How pleasant
the primordial peace, neither true nor false, to a soul
that in the spring

is unemancipated and unopened! After
seventy years of gestation what an illustrious,
stupendous, grand and majestic something
may be brought forth!

The surface of the water becomes a saturated
complexity of blue ripples, while the moss has a dull
green colour like that of olives overlaid with
a shadow of cloud;

the glaucous lichen with its roughened pallor
has conquered the stone; but look at the perfection
of the waters heaping together a motley
of sapphires;

Nonne iam mihi sors suscipiatur?
  Quae scripseram ante hunc saeculi quadrantem,
  cum credere ausus non eram notari
    mi dictata alio

sed putaveram tracta esse meamet
  ex cogitatione, verba prompsi
  antiqua iudex si liceret aequus
    ut legerem senior.

Digna adest quies. Desiderat aulam
  silere veritatis explicator,
  hortatur hortum et ver silere silvam
    crescat ut omne novum.

Digna adest quies. Vult firma patrari
  pax ante ver, pax ante veritatem.
  Placet sedere hic ante codicem artis
    quae latet intus adhuc.

Continet crucis multum diagramma
  croci colore et tulipae libellus.
  Quam prisca oblectat pax, nec ipsa vera
    nec fallax, animam

vere nec manumissam nec apertam!
  Post septuagenarium gerendi
  tempus quod illustre et queat stupendum
    nobile grande pari!

Fluctuum fit aequor caeruleorum
  complexio perfusa, muscus autem
  fusco viret colore tamquam olivae
    quas nube umbra tegit:

glaucus aspero lichen superavit
  pallore saxum: sed freti videte
  perfectionem congerentem acervo
    sapphiros varios:

why should I seek vessels of other colours?
And why should the book necessarily be opened?
Perhaps there's no need to claim what I've
been promised;

for it's implicit in every photon that strikes
the eye that a storm of blossom will
burst forth; it was as much as fifty-eight
years ago

on the East Weares, a wilderness to Portland's
quarrymen, that I freshly bloomed, aroused
by yellow lichen and bright white stone
and a hot summer;

what is it with me and seaside rocks? This
I might reasonably describe as sea, even though
it's stuffed with tiny islands and tamed
by shallows.

The traveller's hindered by islands and I, though
inactive, by unconventional ideas, I'm choked
by the depth of the waves being hardly sufficient
for my soul,

but creation, divine productivity, is contained
unheard and hidden in my heart. With sacred voice
I shan't prophesy things to come, but speak of what time
has already brought.

cur petam colorum ollas aliorum?
   Vel cur libellus debeat recludi?
   Fortasse non necesse vindicare est
     quae promissa habui:

namque conditur photone oculum omni
   pellente partus floreae procellae:
   denos abhinc iam sexies duobus
     annos sepositis

vastitate in Eoa lapicidae
   Portlandiensis florui citatus
   lichene flavo candidaque rupe
     aestate et calida:

rupibus marinis et mihi quid sit?
   Prudenter hoc sat dicerem mare esse
   etsi frequentatum insulis minutis
     ac domitum brevibus.

Insulae viatorem impediuntque
   me notiones desidem insolentes:
   suffocor altitudine aestuum aegre
     sufficiente animae:

at creatio, divina poësis,
   inest inaudita atque operta cordi.
   Futura vates non canam: loquar quae
     tempora iam tulerint.

In Kungsholmen Square

The meaning is conveyed by the words alone
and cannot be brought out in other words
or in more words or in fewer words.
You have to get to know what the words

are to mean, you have so to trust the strength
of the author that his understanding
may be able to overcome discordances
more effectively for you reading.

Learn to do this: but if you choose to shun
the author as an enemy, or even more
mistakenly as an adjudicator, you will fall
prey to unhelpful hostility towards

the meaning of the verses that has to be
sought out, and you will fear, whether
willingly or unwillingly, that the meaning
is hostile towards yourself. Think rather

of the author not as a judge but as
an interpreter skilled in making known
water and churches and houses
and trees and indeed the people.

Meaning is hardly what we might want
to call simple, but the way we ingest it
we can call simple; dare to open
yourself; you're an infinite vessel and

therefore however complex the sense
of the poem may be, it still can't
fill you up: as it is ever more
extensive, so is your own capacity.

In Foro Insulae Regalis

Sententia unis traditur vocabulis:
    expromitur modo istis
nec pluribus nec forte paucioribus:
      significanda decet

te noscere auctorisque sic potentiae
    confidere ut legenti
auctoris intellectus auctius queat
      vincere discidia.

Hoc disce: contra si tibi auctorem arceas
    hostem, vel aggravato
errore forte iudicem, fies malae
      praeda inimicitiae

erga petendam versuum sententiam,
    ergaque temet illam
nolens volens vereris adversariam.
      Auctorem potius

non arbitrantem sed putes interpretem
    enuntiare doctum
aquas et aedes et domos et arbores
      nonnihil ac populum.

Aegre vocemus simplicem sententiam,
    modum sed hauriendi:
aude patere: vas es infinitum et hinc
      quantumcumque licet

sit involuta carminis sententia
    nunquam tamen repleris:
ut semper illa, semper est capacitas
      amplior ipsa tua.

On the Northern Bank of Lake Mälaren

The letter killeth, the Spirit maketh duly
alive, it's time for the Spirit to supersede
the letter. Nature has marked the icon with
her very self; the tulip or crocus which

before obeyed the constraints of geometry's numbers
will soon in the springtime grow with a beauty that isn't
uniform. The bloom is degree and sign
enough; in a puny letter you meet with death.

Yet words themselves are fundamentally not
exactly transparent. The burden of speech is borne
on a formless stretcher that varies according to whatever
the time and the place and the people carry within them.

Consider words not as overlords or judges
but as tiny friends; be defiant with regulations
but embrace the Spirit. Don't you get a sense
today of a more vigorous well-being,

so that your joints now cause you less discomfort,
author-poet and single reader reading?
O you abundant fount and channel of emblems,
hold fast to the faith that good is what will emerge.

Apud Litus Septentrionale Lacus Maelaris

Littera mortem affert, dat Spiritus ordine vitam:
    huic occupare est tempus illius locum.
        Natura semet iconem notavit:
            tulipa sive crocus,

ante geometriae numeris qui paruit aequis,
    mox vere forma crescet haud aequabili.
        Satis gradus est flos satisque signi:
            litterula moreris.

Ipsa tamen sunt verba parum fundamine clara:
    enorme ferculum est loquendae sarcinae,
        dispar secundum temporum ac locorum
            ingenium atque hominum.

Ne dominos neve arbitros sed verba ut amicos
    habe pusillos provocaque regulas
        at Spiritum amplectare. Nonne sentis
            plus hodie vegetae

integritatis ut inde molestent te minus artus,
    auctor poëta et lector unice legens?
        Emblematum fons uber et canalis,
            crede bonum fieri.

UNHESITATING LOVE:
AN EVENING MEDITATION

Having made the world God himself was content and loved it;
dear to me coming in ignorance were the rites
of the Orthodox community living in Oxford;
but now I don't choose to dwell on such weighty cases.

Most beautiful was what power divine gave birth to,
and I've often sung praise of beauty in my poems,
which before or after my death the court of letters
will tear to bits if they think them well-made and worth reading,

but only deem pleasant (if I as a bard may prophesy)
step by step, sluggishly – writing that's somewhat new
seeming rather intractable. In my early youth
it happens to be just Horace that strikes me with dread,

and I've hardly yearned, in my trembling, to open his works.
I pick up a book by chance, a page is soon visible,
I spy these free-flowing, new to me words: "It was night
and up in the sky" – as if I've been hitherto thrust

away from Horace's hingeless confronting door,
but admitted now that I turn up with a ticket;
the key-card is in my fist, I'm therefore invited
to taste and enjoy all the rest of what he has created.

As a pupil and as a teacher alone at my job
having known days both of ease and of difficulty,
I confess myself willingly given over to school,
where adult and child I've spent nearly all my life;

though at the beginning in inconsolable tears
just four years old, and lying prostrate in a corner
of a room that was held in check by a lady called Cook,
in no way could I declare I loved education.

De Non Haesitante Amore: Meditatio Vespertina

Tellurem ipse Deus factam contentus amavit:
   dilexi veniens officia inscius
      coetus Oxoniensis orthodoxi:
sed nunc tam gravibus mihi casibus haud placet studere.

  Formosissima erant peperit quae diva potestas,
    ac formam cecini saepe poëmatis,
       quae si compta putet legique digna
ante aut post obitum discerpserit aula litterarum,

   quae (si vaticiner) mea carmina grata gradatim
    cunctanter statuet, namque habiles parum
       scripturae modice novae videntur.
Me valde iuvenem modo Horatius afficit pavore

   cuius vix operas trepidans aperire cupivi.
    Tollo forte librum, pagina mox patet,
       ignota aspicio soluta verba
quae sunt "Nox erat et caelo" velut antea repulsus

   sim de proposita porta sine cardine Flacci
    iamque admissus habens advena tesseram:
       pugno pignus inest, vocatus ergo
degustare queo tot cetera quot creavit ille.

   Me tam discipulus quam solus in arte magister
    passus difficiles ac faciles dies
       ludo confiteor datum libenter,
in quo paene fui vitam puer atque adultus omnem:

   ast in principio, flens natus quattuor annos
    insolabiliter stratus in angulo
       conclavis domina Coqua subacti,
nequaquam potui me dicere iam scholas amare.

Let's look for a better example of love that will not
delay. The state takes on lots of things, not only
schools but moreover, in this northern land
that's afraid of dangerous hard drink, liquor shops.

A wide-awake salesman living in Sollentuna,
a town not far from the capital, showed on his shelves
a drink that was only allowed to be sent for, which
by law its importer should store until it was asked for.

He received punishment, I was rewarded with something
Torres had pressed, that Iberian firm of renown,
then distilled and withheld for a decade. The drink that was
on offer by chance and got me to give it a try

has a finely complex sweetness I rarely lack
on my tongue when I go to bed, that once found I took
straightaway as a liquid companion. Who'd not like
a companion, who'd not choose to enjoy some comfort?

Behaviour forbidden on principle may be allowed
by special edict. For me it was Tonio Kröger
that gave a reliable proof of this – the boy
portrayed by Thomas Mann at the start of the story.

His sensitiveness is just as great as the beauty
before his eyes. Why mightn't I draw the conclusion
that I too was granted the right to be sensitive
seeing great beauty in some face, some body?

Having grown used to living like that youth an adorer,
on the eighth of September I had arrived in Lübeck
on my travels, but as if I'd been drawn there over
the course of twenty-one years by a favouring godhead.

What film are the Capitol-Lichtspiele (that's the name)
presenting now to one's couple of eyes? I saw
Tonio and his particular friend in black
and white in the place where the author had said they met.

Exemplum melius nihilum cessantis amoris
quaeratur. Publicae plurima sunt rei,
cum ludis etiam, domi Boreae
quae temeta timet temeraria, potuum tabernae.

Sollentunam habitans capiti prope finitimam urbem
ostendit vegetus pegmate venditor
potum quem licuit iubere tantum
mitti, legitime quem conderet invehens petendum.

Poenas ille tulit cepique ego praemia, pressa
a Turrensibus, hoc nomine Hiberico,
dein stillata duo et retenta lustra.
Potus fortuito qui praebitus egit experiri

in lingua cubitans careo dulcedine raro
laute multiplici, ceu comite ilico
adsumpta liquida semel reperta.
Quis non vult comitem, solamine quis negat iuvari?

Quae de principio non sint permissa sinantur
edictis propriis. Indicium mihi
factum Tonius est fidele Caupo,
fabellam expositus Thoma puer incohante Manno.

Tanta huic mollitia est quanta huic ob lumina forma.
Qua re non etiam ius mihi ducere
cessum mollitiae queam videnti
magnam in qua facie, quo corpore pulchritudinem esse?

Sensim suetus ut ille adulescens vivere adulans
octavo Lubecum nactus eram die
Septembris peregrinus at per annos
viginti placito quasi numine tractus huc et unum.

Quam nunc pelliculam praebent ambobus ocellis
Scaenae Lucis, ita est vox, Capitolii?
Vidi Tonium amiculumque terra
pigmento viduos ubi dixerat auctor obvenire.

My thoughts move on to the lithe and beautiful figure
I saw in a car-park in historical Winchester.
We had fetched a group we were going to teach, having turn
and turn about taken leave of a similar one,

and a coach was transporting between the airport and Weymouth's
seaside a very lively crowd. The third
summer after the journey that peaked in Lübeck
was glowing. The drive being half completed now

a welcome pause had been granted. Everyone briefly
escaped the coach. I shall never forget that slender,
nimble figure, so clean and neat in appearance,
with a countenance of such wholesomeness and nobility,

supported by hands that were placed on the tops of seats
packed with young folk as it strove to return to its own
empty one, since as far as feet were concerned
the way was sorely obstructed by piles of luggage.

In the flesh I got to know the figure but slightly –
in palms and fingers. From then on I hardly spoke often
to it where I was born, and even less frequently
later housed in the northern royal city,

but like a rock that had formed after oozing out
of the forge of Vulcan (I've not got closer to Venus)
I witness through crystals retentive in memory: here
is where inner Desire had turned the magnetic needle!

Come pronto, you nectar always prepared to bring healing,
that's not betrayed a wretched man's cheerful hopes.
May the stony, orderly substance of limbs absorb you
and soon lie relaxed. It is time for sleep to pursue me.

Mens procedit ab his in pulchram agilemque figuram
raedarum statione historia probae
visam Vintoniae. Globus docendus
nobis captus erat parili prius invicem relicto

interque aëroportum et Vimutiense vehebat
litus laophorum turbam alacerrimam.
Aestas tertia post iter calebat
cui culmen Lubeci. Mora commoda nunc erat tributa

cursus dimidio completo. Laophorum omnes
evasere brevi tempore. Nunquam ero
oblitus gracilis levis figurae
tam munda specie, tam nobilis ac salubris ore,

sustentae manibus positis in partibus altis
crebrorum iuveni prole sedilium,
conantis vacuum ad suum redire,
obstructo pedibus male tramite sarcinarum acervis.

Perpaulum potui cognoscere carne figuram:
palmis ac digitis. Vix patria mea
illi saepe subinde sum locutus
et posthac etiam minus incola regiae Boreae,

sed sicut lapis e fornace ab origine lapsus
Vulcani (Veneri non propior fui)
crystallo memori tenente testor:
huc magneticam acum converterat intimus Cupido!

Prompte nectar ades semper sanare paratum
nec frustratum hilaras spes miseri viri.
Te substantia saxea ordinata
membrorum bibat ut iaceat cito laxa. Somnus instet.

BRAHMSIAN SCENE

Imagine us sat in a small auditorium
in front of a podium graced with monstrous
lilies and plants with lavish leaves
and drapes and swollen urns and marble;
the air is full of the scent of flowers;
specked with fine dust a single light
flows down through a ceiling window.

A band of musicians enters in no
particular order, and after them
a ruler-straight rank of men whose hair
glistens carefully sculpted beneath their nostrils
and combed away nicely from the pomaded
crowns of their heads; whose starch-stiff collars
hold in place glossy black ties to match
their matt black suits. A large-breasted matron
brings up the rear, resplendent in jewels
and an ornate gown.

What could you find more civilized
than this, further from mountains, sands,
forests, or from states of the heart
that can hardly be borne, forsaken hope,
the lost calling out among abysses?
Yet the woman with comfortable
amiability starts to sing
thus pleasingly:

SCAENA BRAHMSIANA

Sedere parvo nos in auditorio
　　partem finge ante levatam
soli decoram liliis ingentibus
　　　plantisque fronde grandi

velisque et urnis turgidis et marmore:
　　florum implent aëra odores:
lux una tecti per fenestram defluit
　　　pulvisculo micante.

Intrat caterva musicorum errantium,
　　acies dein recta virorum
quibus capilli curiose sculptiles
　　　sub naribus relucent

unctoque pexi suaviter de vertice,
　　quibus et collare amylatum
focale retinet nigrum ad atram synthesem:
　　　mammosa claudit agmen

matrona gemmis clara et ornata stola.
　　Quid cultius hoc reperires,
a monte, harena, saltibus longinquius
　　　affectibusve cordis

vix sustinendis, spe relicta, perditis
　　clamantibus inter abyssos?
Sed comitate commoda cantare sic
　　　orditur illa amoene:

"But who away to one side is that?
His path will soon vanish among the bushes.
The thorn snaps back with a crack when he
has passed. The grass springs up again.
A trackless wilderness devours him."

Sweeter than grapes or plums or pears
in theatrical manner the woman's voice
expresses the plight of one who is wretched
beyond belief – and nobody finds it
believable.

"Ah, say what hands of remedy, say
what hands might bring a cure for torment
to one for whom balm is poisonous, who
from a superabundance of love has only
drunk hatred of humanity?"

She makes a slight pause in her sighing; the deeper
instruments leave off; then the singing
starts up again with a plainer sound,
quiet and sad.

"Just as he used to be despised
he is now a despiser, indulging himself
but unsatisfied in his need for relief,
anxiety secretly gnawing away
at his remaining sense of honour."

It is beautiful; the actor-like mode
delights our hearts like the false depiction
of a beast that has never crawled except
on the paths of myth and lacks all truth;
such a beast must be protected by varnish
and a frame of noble opulence
against the sky, winds, hail, rain, snow
and forces that cannot be tamed.

"At quisnam a latere est? In frutices semita mox sua
vanescit. Crepitu post resilit praeteritus vepres.
Herbae restituunt se. Vorat hunc avia vastitas."

    Mulieris uvis dulcior, prunis, piris
        vox exprimit arte theatri
    afflictionem nemini dignam fide
        praeter fidem miselli.

"Ah dic quae cruciatum illius, ah quae medicae manus
sanent, balsama cui virus habent quique odium modo
humani generis de saturis hausit amoribus?"

    Subsistit illa paululum suspiriis:
        gravia instrumenta quiescunt:
    sonat resumptus deinde cantus planior
        tranquillus atque tristis.

"Ante ut spretus erat, spretor in hoc tempore factus est,
indulgens sibi sed se cupidum non satis adlevans,
clam rodatur honor cui reliquus sollicitudine."

    Pulchrum est: oblectat pectus histricus modus
        ut imago falsa animalis
    tantum vagati fabularum semitis
        et veritate egentis:

    imaginem resina talem protegat
        opulentaque nobilis ora
    contra Iovem, auras, grandinem, imbres ac nivem
        nunquamque vim domandam.

"Si psalteria habent diva tonum quem miser audiat,
ipsi large Pater cor recrea: nubila differens
fontes mille siti trans sterilem maestitiam exhibe!"

"If divine psalteries have a note
that he in his misery can hear,
then grant, O bountiful Father, his heart
new life; disperse the clouds and across
the desolation bring forth a thousand
springs for his thirst."

As soon as the men's choir joins in the singing
harmony comes into being between
the spirits of hall and nature – the concord
of healing at one with its own disease.

God now called upon, surely all matters
of doubt should be resolved? The performance
ends, to use musicianly terms,
in the plagal cadence of confirmatory
amens after the prayers of the church.
Such reverence is too uncomplicated;
when the scene is done there are many things
about which one may have one's own ideas.

Choro virorum instante demum carmini
    symphonia fit geniorum
aulaeque naturaeque: cum morbo suo
    sanationis una.

Deo vocato nonne debent omnia
    dubitata repente resolvi?
Concentus exit, ut loquuntur musici,
    cadentia plagali

firmantis amen post preces ecclesiae.
    Nimis est reverentia simplex:
scaena peracta multa sunt de quis licet
    cepisse opinionem.

TRUTH AS POEM

Or could pure simple truth, not yet recounted
to any listener, be taken for a whole
poem? The undaubed for a picture or
the stoneless for a statue all complete?

Can what's been called surreal come into being
without involving thinking and no dreams dreamt,
or what the princes of Serendip met with
without fate having delights in store?

Can signs exist of such grand circumstance
as to compel belief beyond all scruple,
which afterwards lack any worth as signs,
and omen excepted are quite devoid of content?

My brother's name has no connection with
my own name, even if both of them are read
just where the venerable life of Saint Paul
is chronicled within the New Testament's pages.

Rarely has my brother's patron been given
a place in coloured windows, and my own
is only slightly more common. A church that once
was Anglican but now belongs to the Pope,

anointed in its name by the Blessed Trinity,
joined long ago for the eyes of Dorchester people
these patrons as glass in its wall; there set on the left
is mine and the other is close to it on the right.

But what you've not yet learnt, good reader, is
that before I discovered this singular state of affairs
my heart had taken a shine as it were to a voice
in skin and bone called out from the list of the prophets.

Velut Carmen Veritas

An velut carmen queat ipsa totum
sola veritas haberi nemini narrata adhuc?
    An velut pictura quod haud litum est vel
        sine saxo statua integra?

Fitne quod dixere superreale
cogitatione omissa, somniis absentibus,
    quodve noscebant domini Serendip
        sine fatis hilarantibus?

Suntne tam grandi gravitate signa
quae fidem cogant tributam praeter omnem scrupulum,
    postea quae signa carent valore,
        super omen sat inania?

Copula haud nomen ligat ulla fratris
cum meo, licet legantur paginis intra Novum
    ambo Testamentum ubi vita Pauli
        memoratur venerabilis.

Fratris est raro positus patronus
in coloratis fenestris, paululum frequentior
    est meus: templum prius Anglicanum,
        modo Papae tamen obsequens,

Trinitate unctum titulo Beata,
iam diu vitro patronos Durnovariensibus
    iunxit in muro: situs est sinistra
        meus, alter prope dextera.

At quod ignoras, bone lector: ante
singularem rem repertam cor meum dilexerat
    ex prophetarum numero vocatam
        quasi vocem cute et ossibus.

Its parents had got it a name one never hears:
its guardian in the sweet choir of heavenly beings
is never found depicted in any image
except as one in the company of many.

Be amazed with me now, since this compelling voice
can be seen – and lest you misunderstand, the wall
and church are the same – four paces to the left,
and similar to the pair already mentioned.

Shouldn't I think this a portent of the future,
that leaving my former home I'd been fated to make
my way from here to an unknown east, just as
those steps bring one closer to the holy altar?

Shouldn't I think the voice had been doomed a century
back to welcome me and make me its friend?
What ensue are pain and ponderings
that send me off on a venturesome course;

however the voice is soon silent and fades away.
Why? Perhaps because of my groundless pride,
procrastinating sloth or inadequate will –
such was I. D'you get the poem? Can you explain
the story? You've insight, you're learning enough of the facts:
you're journeying out in the pressed-in world of art.

Huic inauditum tulerant parentes
nomen: hanc tutela curans caelitum in dulci choro
    non repraesentatur imagine unquam
        nisi multis comitantibus.

Nunc stupe mecum, quoniam videtur –
perperam ne comprehendas, murus idem est, templum idem –
    quattuor laevum gradibus priori
        similis vox subigens pari.

Nonne portentum rear hoc futuri,
me lare antiquo relicto destinatum ut tenderem
    hinc ad incompertum orientem ut arae
        propius pes graditur sacrae?

Nonne vocem illam rear ante saeclum
obligatam quae salutet meque amicum seligat?
    Fit dolor, fiunt meditationes
        quibus audax init impetus:

attamen vox mox silet ac liquescit.
Cur? Meae fortasse causa futtilis superbiae,
otii procrastinantis vel voluntatis levis –
sic fui. Noscisne carmen? Explicasne fabulam?
    Iam sapis, de re satis erudiris:
        iter artis facis artibus.

Things at the Same Time both Plain and Obscure

Mighty Creator, "Or could pure simple"
has been written, but I've not completed a candid
report of such cases. Is there a point
in you sending me incomprehensible signs?

Or ought I to twig these things come from the devil?
Wouldn't the trickster reward me to make
my deception more heinous, more swift, more easy?
So even the evil one grants no decipherment?

The nature of pledges we don't understand
till they're kept and the secrets are ours to enjoy:
or do you already grant what you've promised
unbeknownst to us? Grim the enigma remains.

Here's an example: why do all four houses
I've lived for some time in sport ordinal symbols
that amount to the heptad in front of doors
not used to the irksome noise of traffic?

As a child I was conscious of Weymouth being
the town of my birth and at fifty-two Southview
Road I grew up there: since then the row's
been extended and now the number's another:

emerging one stands on the then neglected
lowest stump of Emmadale Road,
from which were reached only, established for citizens
stricken by war, small plots to grow food in.

At seventy-nine Granby Close however,
a street doing well on only one exit,
I spent adolescence until it was time
for the sake of studies to abandon home.

Simul Evidentia atque Obscura

O Creator potens, "An velut carmen" est
scriptum, at haud exacta talium casuum
candida relatio. Per signa quae carent
intellegibilitate ecquid effeceris?

Aut debeamne res scire esse diaboli?
Nonne ille dolosus me remuneretur
ut magis decipiar, ocius, facilius?
Nec malo donetur interpretatio?

Antequam servantur atque nos abditis
fruemur promissa non comprehendimus:
quaeve pollicitus es iamne das, quae tamen
haud noscimus? Restat aenigma molestum.

Ut exemplum feram, domorum quattuor
ubi habitavi diu cur symbolum ordinis
heptadi quaeque gerit aequum ante ianuam
strepitui vehiculorum insuetam inimico?

Vimutium erat satus oppidum puerulo,
crevique ibi quinquagesima secunda
Viae Prospectuum nomine Australium:
auctiore serie nunc numerus alius est:

insistit exeuns infimo termino
Emmivallis Viae tempore hoc neglecto
unde modo in hortulos adibatur holerum
bello dolentibus statutos civibus.

At adulescentulus septuagesimo
nono domicilio Clausi remorabar
Grambiensis uno felicis exitu
dum reliqui larem causa studiorum.

Later in Stockholm I occupied rooms
located in Bredgränd in the Old City;
an archway beside the door I made use of,
the seventh, allows pedestrians egress.

Thereafter my home has been in the edifice
of thirty-four Tomtebogatan, in front
of whose entrance cars turn with slanting wheels
and retreat, unable to travel further,

for in that charming Parisian way
which always gives pleasure to visitors, steps
at the end lead down to a lower terrace
amid the shadows of sun-basking trees.

Mysteries coming in sevens is standard:
so must I feel awe? Or induce it myself?
My path be hemmed in by silence and loneliness
without a friend's warmth to console and support me?

Let anyone minded check what I've been saying,
without any problem he'll prove it the truth;
now I must deal with some strange undergoings
to which I alone, the song's maker, can testify.

Swedes know zilch of the date upon which
the Orthodox celebrate flowery Easter;
why a notable vision revealed itself
four times on this day I can't explain.

What sort of vision? A tall-grown ephebe,
lithe and quite lean and quite gentle of aspect,
not often glimpsed, as if held back by shyness,
a neighbour whose building was almost next-door.

Ought I to sing him in hendecasyllables,
whose aptest star-sign would be the Twins?
There on the ground floor builders buy battens:
what baton's to hand with which to conduct myself?

Holmiae serius conclavia habebam
Urbis sita Lato Veteris Angiporto:
fornix prope ostium quod mihi erat usui
septimum permittit egredi pedestres.

Deinde tricesimo quarto domus fuit
aedificio Viae Nidi Geniorum:
ante portam rotis vertuntur obliquis
reveniuntque raedae pergere impeditae,

nam more venusto qui Parisiorum
Lutetiae placet semper peregrinis
fine descenditur scalis ad inferum
aggerem inter umbras apricarum arborum.

Occurrere arcana communis est locus
septena: terrearne aut ipse terream?
Semitane saepta sit solo silentio
sine sinu solante sublevante amici?

Narrata quicumque cupidus examinet,
veridica valebit monstrare commode:
experimenta iam mira tractanda sunt
unico teste me versuum poëta.

Suetici nil sciunt de diebus in quis
orthodoxi Pascha floridum celebrent:
explicare nequeo cur quater nobilis
hoc die visio se revelaverit.

Visio qualis haec? Procerus ephebus
agilis et gracilior blandiorque facie,
conspectus haud saepe quasi pudore inhibitus,
propemodum proximis vicinus aedibus.

Syllabisne undecim recinere illum decet,
cui sit aptissimum sidus Geminorum?
Illic pedeplanis structore regulae
emuntur: norma mihi quae suppeditatur?

At Easter, salvation-tide, the sudden duty
of joyous delirium in faithful submission
is laid upon Christians that two days before
in faithful submission had orders to grieve.

In my heart I'm always both cheerful and mournful;
my spirit's unable to change in an instant,
though often it's tried, and guilts both for joy
and for misery tear my bowels to shreds.

I feel your forgiveness but doubt all the same,
not having forced through sufficient repentance
or believed enough that grace could cleanse me,
knowing myself to be all too evil.

Too little bendable, I've not obeyed enough,
having too little supposed that you've wanted
my own special aptitude wiped out, my will
broken, me frozen by a gloomy conscience.

What, Lord, do you want of me? More than candour,
through-and-through honesty, what can I offer you?
In times of crisis you brought me a vision –
or at least a vision was brought me from somewhere –

when my soul had most and with sharpest pain
despaired of itself, on the same holy day
four times in one lustrum, indeed from the fourth
to the eighth of the current millennium's years.

Is the vision shown trite and trivial? Should it
be obvious here is no meaning, my mind
revealed moreover as run-of-the-mill,
vulgar and wanting, silly and dull?

Do I need to be shown that signs are imbued
with falsehoods and only your love, kept safe
in my intellect even though often it can't
be felt in my breast, is worthy my trust?

Salutis tempus est Pascha subitumque onus
gravat Christianos obsequente ex fide
hilaris amentiae quamquam ante triduum
obsequente ex fide iubebantur angi.

Corde semper simul laetor et lugeo:
spiritus non valet statim mutare se –
saepe conatus est – visceraque distrahit
tam culpa gaudii quam culpa miseriae.

Te dedisse veniam sentio sed simul
sum dubius: haud satis paenitentiam egi,
non satis credidi me posse gratia
perlui, me nimis novi nefarium.

Non satis flexilis non satis oboedio,
namque voluisse te non satis putavi
indolem destrui, voluntatem meam
frangi, gelare me conscientiam atram.

Quid Domine vis mihi? Num queo dare tibi
ingenuitate plus, veritate tota?
Discriminis horis visionem mihi
tulisti, visiove undecumque lata est,

anima cum maxime diffisa erat sibi
pessimeque acerbe, lustro quater uno
iisdem feriis, quarto videlicet
chiliadis ad octavum instantis ab anno.

Visane est visio trita et trivialis?
Sitne planum per hanc nil significari
sed ostendi meam mentem ordinariam,
vulgarem et indigam, stultam et improvidam?

Docendumne est esse signa fallaciis
imbuta solumque mea fiducia
dignum amorem tuum certum in animo meo,
quem tamen percipere nequit saepe pectus?

And in a certain so murky November,
on a quite different day of acknowledged guilt
and insufficiency, while in my brain
I carried proof of my wilful nature,

the infrequent vision, the ephebe that for ages
my eyes had rarely caught sight of, boarded
the very bus chance had me travelling on –
this occasion surely held some message?

An olympiad's passed since the latest of such
apparitions. I guess that the young man has moved,
but here I stay, picked for an omen and grudged
its rewards, all this time under disapprobation.

Quodamque Novembri tam tenebricoso
prorsus alio die noxiae cognitae
et infirmitatis, cum contumaciae
indicationem cerebro tenebam,

infrequens visio, tempore satis amplo
rarus oculis meis conscendit ephebus
in laophorum egomet quo forte vehebar:
in occasione hac nonne sit nuntius?

Est ex epiphania tali novissima
praeterita olympias. Migravisse duco
iuvenem, at hic remaneo, selectus omini
nec ratus praemiis, adhuc improbatus.

AN UNDANKBARE GEBER

Ovid hat auch auf getisch gedichtet. Was dachten
die Geten? Lucidor leckte mit sieben Zungen,
nicht nur mit der schwedischen. Durch die Jahrhunderte
haben Gelehrte und andere Bildungsopfer
lateinisch sowohl wie einheimisch kommuniziert.

Hopkins versuchte walisische Verse zu schreiben.
Auf französisch kicherte Eliot unbekümmert.
Für George genügte nicht Sprachen zu entleihen,
er hat eine neue romanische Mundart entworfen.
Schön floß Tolkiens erfundenes Elfenreden.

Galizisch taugte im spanischen Mittenalter
für Liebesgesänge besser als kastilisch:
Rosalía hat es neu aufgeweckt und errichtet.
Gleichzeitig erhob William Barnes mit Bauernkraft
seine *Dorset Speech* zur Sphäre der Litteratur.

Lorca aus Andalusien wurde genötigt,
eigene galizische Strophen zusammenzuklecksen.
Nach langer Reise stellte sich Nabokov
eine unmißverständlich falsche Sprache vor,
seinen Kinbote als unbefriedigend anzudeuten.

Pessoa übersetzte Bottos *Canções*
vortrefflich ins Englische, komponierte aber
selber auf englisch oft mittelmäßig und manchmal
direkt abscheulich: leider war sein Trieb
gelegentlich stärker als seine Selbsterkenntnis.

Auf Mark, die ich nicht beherrsche, trete ich auch
wie diese Sprachenentdecker, aber öfter
(und nicht nur wenn ich dichte), ohne zu wissen
warum – wozu – ob Erfolg um die Ecke lauere.
Suche ich, ist das Gesuchte unerkennbar…

AD INGRATOS DATORES

Et Getica Ovidius fecit exsul carmina.
Quid censuerunt ibi Getae? Septem asperis
linguis nec una Lucidorus Suetica
lambit rogantem litteras. Per saecula

sunt eruditi victimaeque alii scholae
aeque locuti vocibus vernaculis
atque hac Latina. Manlius conatus est
Hopcinsius conficere versus Cambrice.

Francorum Eliotus sibi cachinnavit levis
ex ore. Notos sed Georgeio modos
Stephano loquendi mutuari vix satis:
aluit recentem de Latinis surculis.

Fluxit venuste Tolcienii mythica
ficte loquela. Putata Medio vox erat
Gallaeca in Aevo commodior Hispanico
cantibus amoris: suscitavit denuo

Rosalia et illam erexit. In eodem die
Barnesius Gulielmus idioma intulit
vi rustica quondam humile Dorsetiae suae
in nemus Apollinare. Voluit Baetica

ex arida Lorca ipse colere idyllia
Gallaeca. Post iter amplius Nabuchides
fallacem aperte linguam imaginatus est
Cinbota ut exlex reciperetur perfidus.

Persona Ferdinandus induit optime
Botti poëmata vocem in Anglicam, tamen
suapte panxit Anglice mediocriter
vel admodum odio: maior interdum quidem

illi voluntas quam sui prudentia.
In terram et ego mihi non regendam transeo
ut transierunt hi repertores novae
loquacitatis, sed putem frequentius,

Trotzdem fange ich an zu verstehen, vermuten.
In Wartesälen und Spirituosenläden
und anderwärts in Schweden liest man oft
ohne eigentliche Erklärung, wieviele Leute
da zwischen jenen Wänden sich sammeln dürfen.

Wer das bestimme, und welche für das Nachleben
dieser Verordnung wohl verantwortlich seien,
davon wird nichts gesagt. Kaum will man glauben,
da jeder Besucher die übrigen rechnen soll,
verpflichtet, das anzumelden, was nicht stimmt.

Ich schreibe, mich dünkt es, als schlage ich Notizen an,
die ähnlicherweise ohne Kontext gelesen
werden. In diese Lokale zugelassen
und sozusagen amtlich als Poet bekränzt
deklamiere ich nur zwecklos und formell.

Ihr begreift gar nicht, die ihr die Notizen lest –
die meine Stimme unter den eurigen hört –
wie unbedingt ein Geber erlauben muß,
daß der arme Empfänger irgend eine Erstattung
anbiete, wenn diese auch ganz lächerlich scheine.

Wie möchte ich euch meiner Dankbarkeit Größe zeigen,
Lateiner, Deutschen, Franzosen, Portugiesen,
wenn ich nicht unter euch irren und lauten dürfte?
Auch für Großmütige gelten Obliegenheiten:
auch ihr seid im Dankbarkeitswirrwarr hilflos verwickelt.

nec semper ubi meditatus adsum scrinio,
incognitis ratione, meta, pignore,
laeti probabilitate serius exitus.
Quod expetivi non sciatur ad manum.

Nihilo minus comprendere incipio, statum
conspicere rerum. Sueticis in atriis
publicis et aliis, oenopoliis quoque,
sine explicatione disquirentibus

proscribitur quot liceat homines congredi
inter parietes. Capere non conceditur
quis iubeat aut cui forte munus incubet
exerceatur norma curandi loco.

Scribo, vel est sic visa res, quasi quamlibet
proscriptionem more proponam pari
sine veritatis vi, sine cohaerentia
animis aperta ceteris. Admissus huc

laurosque ut ita dicatur artis vatium
ritu nec optione vulgi promerens
recito sine sono vel malevoli spe soni
aut comis. Hos utcumque legitis futtiles

titulos meamve auditis inter proprias
vocem, parum tenetis heu quam debeant
simpliciter omnes sinere dantes libere
tunc recipientem offerre miserum quae queat

gratae memoriae signa, quamquam haec forsitan
videantur illudenda. Quomodo pectoris
ostendam abundavisse laetitiam omnibus
vobis, Latinis, Lusitanis, incolis

Germaniaeque Galliaeque, ni sinar
paulum vagari canereque inter vos? Valet
et largientibus obligatio: simul
vinclum benignos ac beatos impedit.

THE ICON OF SAINTS FLORUS
AND LAURUS

To Saints Florus and Laurus

With blows upon stone a temple was being made
for the gods, but the beats of the hearts in the breasts of both,
O steadfast pair, rang out with the voice of a new,
    a beaten Master, and so you were driven

at the chisel's strokes to receive the invincible Cross.
Stone and men that had been bound by an age
of lies were aroused, given shape and hallowed; the people
    were renewed in their spirits, the temple too

in its title; building and village acknowledged Christ
as their lord. However you were seized and thrown
into an ancient well and there abandoned.
    The well was sealed. No more was the country

cultivated, no more the realms of the mind;
no wisdom promoted formation of any kind;
but this great achievement of yours lived on retold
    in the mouths of men: nor did your achievement

die in the bowels of earth: for the rock of your unhewn
sepulchre suddenly broke itself open; the water
of life flowed forth from a disregarded cranny;
    horses gather simply in order

to drink here from your refreshing stream; the wards
of a new age recollect your ancient renown;
your bones are raised from their bed that they may be honoured,
    while all around an untamed tribe

of horses frolic uncurbed by iron bits
and free from harsh bridles enjoy a verdant meadow
of Eden. Truth is here plainly shown reborn,
    as if it were a beautiful dream.

ICON SANCTORUM FLORI ET LAURI

Ad Sanctos Florum et Laurum

Ictibus in lapidem fiebat aedes dis data:
sed cordis ictus, o pii, utriusque in pectore vestrum
    icti Magistri voce resonabant recentis,
        invictamque Crucem

accipere in scalpri impetibus adigebamini.
Sunt lapis et homines conciti quos mendax vinxerat aevum,
    sculpti, sacrati: populus est animo novatus,
        templum etiam titulo:

imperium Christi agnovit et constructio
et vicus. Estis vos tamen prensati, praecipitati
    deinde in vetustum puteum et illic derelicti.
        Occlusus puteus.

Non iam rus, non iam mentis colebantur loca:
formationem quamlibet sapientia nulla movebat:
    sed facinus optimum adusque vivebat relatum
        hoc vestrum ore hominum,

nec vestrum gremio terrae facinus hoc mortuum est:
quassata namque repente sunt non caesi saxa sepulcri,
    fluxitque vitae lympha ab oblito recessu:
        congrediuntur equi

ut modo aquas vestras refrigerantes hic bibant:
famam recordantur novae antiquam aetatis alumni:
    tolluntur ossa verenda vestra de cubile
        dum fera equina tribus

lascivit circum soluta frenis ferreis
durisque habenis libera prato viridante iuvatur
    Eden. Renata hic veritas plane docetur
        somnia pulchra imitans.

To God the Son

What kind of temple was it that you prepared
for us, God? Your image, no more? Your simple unique
image should seem sufficient, but down and in thither
    you swept, you willingly entered the last

dark depths of matter's shaft and arrived at the end,
were shattered, destroyed, and suffered the gainful death
of martyrdom. Death would have liked to be able to laugh,
    but unimpaired martyrdom lived on.

What sort of rock was it then that you split apart?
Our sluggish and speechless body. You broke the long
coursing of aeons through all as yet untouched ages:
    you lightened the plight of the man who tills

the land, who is heavily punished with duties of labour,
granting him water unbucketed, corn unscythed
and milk without stables, honey with no painful bees.
    All flesh is grass. but no reaping-hook threatened.

To mankind that languished in empty stupor you came
and gave us feeling, filled us: the phantom received
your showering Godhead; that seamless work of yours
    intact, this human garment, you tore

asunder; the Styx you parted in twain beneath
the skiff of hell, thus halted; you deprived
the heavens of all their light, that it bounteously given
    might gladden us as we wept in darkness;

the veil of the temple was rent from top to threshold;
at the same time the earth was shaken. The order has been
blotted out that used to rule everything; we who are guilty
    have all been granted a strange forgiveness.

Ad Deum Filium

Quale Deus templum nobis parasti? Num tui
imaginem nec plus? Satis mera debeat unica imago
　　tui videri, tamen es interlapsus illuc,
　　　　materiaeque libens

obscuram intrasti imam cavernam, nactus es
finem, peremptus, dirutus ac martyrium utile passus.
　　Ridere voluit Mors, tamen vivebat usque
　　　　martyrium incolume.

Qualem autem lapidem tu diffidisti? Nostrum iners
infansque corpus. Omnia longum per saecula cursum
　　aeonum adhuc intacta rupisti: levasti
　　　　agricolam officio

punitum graviter laboris absque hamis aqua,
sine falce Cerere et lacte ibi stabulum qua deest, sine acerbis
　　melle apibus. Omnis est caro faenum, minata
　　　　nulla tamen secula.

Venisti vacuo stupore ad homines languidos
nos redditurus sensiles, plenos: phantasma recepit
　　tuum profusum numen: intactum scidisti
　　　　inconsutile opus,

hanc hominis tunicam: tu separavisti Stygem
cymba sub Orci iam stata: lucem omnem surripuisti
　　caelorum ut hilararemur illa largienda
　　　　flentes in tenebris:

discessit velum templi deorsum ad limina:
commota tellus est simul. Ordo prius omne gubernans
　　deletus est semel: omnibus data mira nobis
　　　　sontibus est venia.

To Humanity and to the Guardian Angel of Eden

That world beknown to humans through faith alone
harmonizes with this which is fit for our senses. An ether's
rainbow joins the two like a bridge, for the workshop
        must harmonize with the work that appears.

Can you bear such harmony? Or is the act of the play
a meaningless babble so long as concord prevails?
Humanity, speak: is the hymn a whoopee of hypocrisy,
        faith nauseatingly trite and flat?

Hoof-flattened and worn is the path of the slow, dull herd;
well, the beasts had long before drunk from the sacred spring;
by his doing before mankind the Almighty caused nature
        to arise and approved the grand artefact;

had divine approbation made a blunder? Matter
is saturated with embryos of the wondrous
and unexpected, for any square inch of the covering
        of every item conceals a power

able to loose here the leathern thongs from the shafts
of the wagon of penal labour. With excellent timing
the Word will return to us; already the earth
        has begun to quake. The strictness of law

every quark can abolish, and thus can miracles happen.
Permit us to enter now, radiant guardian of Paradise.
Our dress is unsuitable, so is the state of our hair;
        of the fact that a marriage-feast has been

going on we are ignorant, having construed the announcement
up to now rather vaguely and not very fittingly. Let not
the plank break asunder on which we might gain salvation:
        let not our irreverence in times past

decide the outcome. An end is here offered which every
suckling born would opt for. Us who are captive
ensnared may the icon of freedom receive! Turn away
        the implacable flame of your fiery sword!

Ad Homines atque ad Angelum Custodem Eden

Consonat ille homini fiducia modo cognitus
huic mundus habili sensibus. Ut pons ligat aetheris ambos
arcus, quod officina debet consonare
cum parente opere.

Consona quae sic sunt vosne toleratis? Anne fit
inepta cantilena dum concordia praevalet actu?
Estne hymnus, homines, orgia adsimulationis,
taetre trita fides?

Trita via est pecorum torpore tardorum ungulis:
animalia autem iam diu biberant ab origine sancta:
natura oborta est homine prior opera Supremi
grande probantis opus:

num fallax fuerat divina comprobatio?
Materia satura est germinum mirabilis atque inopini,
nam tegminis rerum omnium quaevis quadrata
occulit uncia vim

solvere quae valeat temone lorum scorteum
laboris hic poenarii. Mature venerit ad nos
Verbum illud iterum: iam solum pavere coepit.
Tollere quodque potest

duritiam legis quarcum itaque licet accidere
miranda. Nos admitte nunc, Paradisi splendide custos.
Vestimur haud bene, comimur non bene capillos,
non intellegimus

processisse dapes hic nuptiales, nuntium
interpretati sumus adhuc incertius ac minus apte.
Ne tabula corrumpatur in qua sospitemur:
ne vetus impietas

eventum statuat. En finem oblatum hic omnibus
optandum alumnis editis. Laqueis nos libera captos
icon recipiat! Non piandam averte flammam
igniferi gladii!

A Song for the Varangian Martyrs

O holy martyrs, warrior Theodore, John
flower among youths, Varangians who readily
ensured the salvation of the Russians through
the shedding of blood!

Father enlisted by the coasts of the Bosphorus,
baptized in Christ's mystical river, grant
what we shall ask you by the name you have
merited, God's gift.

Brave son of a brave father, radiant
with a fair unblemished body
joined to a pure soul, we pray you
to treat us kindly.

Show both of you favour to your Nordic stock,
mindful of ancient clearings and empty
marshes and the grey sea bearing abroad
troops in abundance.

From either side the far from secure city
of Kiev and your native country praise you,
one a treacherous host, one the enduring
origin of your forbears.

The lords and elders of the people once chose
by lot the chaste youth to be offered to the gods:
you, his father, denied that right can thus
be determined.

"Not gods," you said, "do you have upon your altars,
but sticks of wood which in time will be turned
to dust. Do sticks drink or eat or have the power
to speak with their lips?

In no wise are we helped by hand-made gods:
the one supreme undivided God is he whom
the Greeks worship with magnificent prayers
sung before the Cross.

CARMEN VARANGIANUM

Martyres sancti, Theodore miles,
flos Ioannes iuvenum, Varangi
sponte Russorum tuiti salutem
    sanguine fuso!

Bosphori conscripte parens ad oras,
mystico Christi fluvio lavatus
quae Dei donum merito petemus
    nomine dones.

Fortis a forti generate fili
candidae iuncto sine labe pulchro
corpore effulgens animae, rogamus
    nos bene tractes.

Nordicae stirpi memores favete
pristini saltus, vacuae paludis
ac maris glauci peregre vehentis
    agmina crebra.

Urbs parum secura Chioviae vos,
vos ager natalis utrimque laudant,
hospita haec fallax, patiens origo
    hic atavorum.

Principes olim populi senesque
victimam castum iuvenem deorum
sorte legerunt: genitor negasti
    fas ita cerni.

"Non deos" inquis "sed habetis aris
ligna quae fient aliquando pulvis.
Ligna num potant vel edunt labrisve
    dicere possunt?

Dis manu sculptis minime iuvamur:
unus est summus Deus ille simplex
quem colunt Graeci precibus decoris
    pro cruce cantis.

He created the green earth, gave us the sea
and sky and raised into their orbits
the clear lights of the sun and its twin
the moon.

Moreover Paradise, filled with every
pleasure, acquired for its crown the race,
mighty in generation, of loftily reasoning
mankind.

Man is the earthly likeness of God. Never
would I stand stupidly by and surrender
the son dear to my heart to evil spectres
and demons."

Valiantly, warrior, you resist the abduction,
with equal vigour, boy, you fight at your father's
side: the wild band are unable to perpetrate
this hateful crime:

but while you stand on the planking
above the ladder, weapons strike
the posts beneath your feet and part
of the house falls in.

Through wicked cunning your lives are brought
to an end: by Christ's grace you win everlasting
lives in heaven: may our mortal race steadfastly
follow you.

May we the long disregarded draw as avengers
advantage from the unrequited consequences
of your death and be rightly restored to the better
preserved religion.

May, Theodore, faith and, John, hope now be given
to your people, and may charity never be wanting:
bear your kinsfolk aloft in the company
of the orthodox.

Ille tellurem viridem creavit,
aequor et caelum dedit atque in orbes
solis et lunae geminae levavit
    lumina clara.

Amplius fructu paradisus omni
plenus acquisivit uti coronam
mentibus celsis hominum potentem
    semine prolem.

Est homo terrena Dei figura.
Filium nunquam mihi corde carum
traderem larvis stupidus malignis
    daemonibusque."

Raptui miles validus resistis,
ad latus pugnas puer acer aeque:
hoc nequit taetrum scelus impetrare
    saeva caterva:

sed super scalas tabulatione
stantibus vobis quatiunt columnas
arma sub vestris pedibus domusque
    pars ruit intro.

Per dolum vitae pereunt iniquum:
caelites vitas capitis perennes
gratia Christi: moritura proles
    firma sequatur.

Vindices eventa diu neglecti
mortis usurpemus inulta vestrae:
iure reddamur melius retentae
    religioni.

Nunc fides stirpi Theodore detur,
spes Ioannes, neque desit unquam
caritas: gentem penes orthodoxos
    ferte superne.

WEDDING SONG

O Virgin's Son, our speech
is of God begotten of God
having entered upon this human path.
PRAISE BE TO YOU, O CHRIST,
FRIEND OF THE NUPTIAL BOND.

When you journey to Cana as man,
when you work your first wonder as God,
you are silent concerning Your message.

The hostage still awaits the day
when the redemption prepared for her
shall be bestowed.

With what sorrow the house is ashamed
that cannot give folk celebrating
a marriage whereof to drink!

Moved in her heart Your mother
at once asks Your help
for those in want of drink.

"Are we to have this matter
in common?" You say: "it is not yet
due time for My service."

Nonetheless as a loving son
You willingly grant a famous sign
to the intimate suppliant.

You prevent the thirst of the guests,
disgrace for the household
and our continuing in ignorance.

Then Your parent bids the servants
to do whatever You, an obedient
Commander, may require.

CARMEN NUPTIALE

De Deo genitum Deum
gressum in hanc hominum viam
nate virgine dicimus.
CHRISTE LAUS TIBI COPULAE
    NUPTIALIS AMICO.

Canam iter faciens homo,
mira prima creans Deus,
nuntium retices tuum.

Sperat obses adhuc diem
quo tributa sit illius
apparata redemptio.

Quo dolore pudet domum
quae nequit dare quod bibant
nuptias celebrantibus!

Mota corde petit statim
mater auxilium tuum
potione carentibus.

"Remne consociabimus?"
inquis: "officii mei
hora debita non erat."

Supplici tamen intimae
nobile auspicium libens
filius pius adnuis.

Hospitum prohibes sitim
dedecusque domesticis
nosque pergere nescios.

Dein parens famulos iubet
quod poposceris exsequi
imperator oboediens.

"Fill the ewers with water, let the master
of the feast taste that he may judge."
They carry away the cup.

The bridegroom is to hear the judgement:
"Wine of such quality has been brought forth,
preferable to that provided earlier!"

Woman is joined to man
just as You, the Good Shepherd,
call forth Your flock of sheep.

You render this path of mankind
one of heavenly beings, trivial things
wonderful, sad matters joys.

Our transitory life is made everlasting,
hunger is assuaged by the best
of sustenance and savour.

For You shall outdo all
that has passed by all
that You keep until the end.
PRAISE BE TO YOU, O CHRIST,
FRIEND OF THE NUPTIAL BOND.

"Vos replete hydrias aqua:
gustet architriclinus ut
iudicet." Calicem ferunt.

Sponsus arbitrium sciet:
"vina qualia prompta sunt
praeferenda prius datis!"

Iungitur mulier viro
sicut upilio bonus
evocas ovium gregem.

Reddis hanc hominum viam
caelitum, trivialia
mira, tristia gaudia.

Vita nostra caduca fit
sempiterna, levat famem
optimus cibus ac sapor.

Namque praeterita omnia
omnibus superaveris
quae tueris in exitum.
CHRISTE LAUS TIBI COPULAE
   NUPTIALIS AMICO.

Saint Wite Tells her Tale

My bones stay put here in the village church,
near where some heathen Danesmen lay at lurch
one evening by the Lyme-to-Bridport way.
No man worth robbing had come riding past,
so when they saw me, "Ah," they thought, "at last!
There'll be a ransom for her friends to pay."
"Let me alone, let me alone," I cried.
    And here I bide.

"Who is your greatest neighbour?" asked a Dane.
"In what direction can we find the thane?
What would he give us not to take your life?
Where is your priest, where are the precious things
he'll use at mass, the people's offerings?"
I told them, "Wealth need have no truck with strife!
Here close at hand is where true riches hide."
    And here I bide.

I led them down the track towards the sea.
Distrustful, muttering they followed me
to where my well was and my simple hut,
its cross lit brightly by the setting sun.
I showed them where my work and prayer were done:
no lack of richness here, indeed a glut!
I said, "You chose an ancress for your guide."
    And here I bide.

They killed me out of anger, nothing more.
What I held dear they had no honour for,
just ignorant contempt and empty hate.
My priest is He for whom all heaven sings,
my lord is no thane but the King of Kings,
my greatest neighbour He who is Most Great.
About where value lies I hadn't lied.
    And here I bide.

Narratio Sanctae Candidae

Etiam ossa rustica aedes tenet hic posita mea
regione qua repleti iacuere malitia
latebris Dani latrones equitum ut bona raperent.
Caruere forte praedis: ego vespere venio
pedibus via Lymensi: capior misera cito.
Danus "obses" inquit "adstat redimenda familia."
"Sinite ire me!" reclamo. Tamen hic ego maneo.

"Locuples quis incolarum est? Ubi dic habitat erus
populo suo fidelis, publica imperia volens?
Ut libereris auri quantum puta numeret?
Ubi retegitur sacerdos, stipis arca beneficae,
pretiosa vasa missae, proba textilia, libri?"
Ego tunc "at haud necesse est scelere impetrare opes,
prope enim reconditae sunt." Tamen hic ego maneo.

Cata tramite antecedo velut inde mare petam
neque me feri sequuntur sine murmure dubio.
Ubi iubare sol obliquo crucem inaurat occidens
puteo casam paratam nanciscimur humilem.
Precibus laboribusque et nihili datur alii
studium meum: quid optem quasi divitis operae?
"Monacham videtis" aio. Tamen hic ego maneo.

Modo me necant in ira: nihil aestimabile
sapiunt, nihil verentur, potius ciet odium
fastidiosum in has res dulcedine saturas.
Erit unicus erus unus Dominus mihi Sabaoth
Pater omnium Creator, Genitusque mea Salus
simul Agnus ac Sacerdos ac Pastor in ovibus,
et Spiritus Animator Paracletus ignifer.
Levius meo nec est nec fieri poterit onus:
habear redempta vere. Tamen hic ego maneo.

There's holiness about our coast and hills
older than any brigand knife that spills
martyr-blood seed for later hands to reap.
Whatever's sacred shan't be moved or mocked:
whatever's noble shan't be rent or rocked:
whatever's ours to cherish shan't go cheap.
For rights and right that can't be budged I died.
    And here I bide.

– You've named a flag for me? I nearly laughed!
Go on then, even if it does seem daft.
If it's for Dorset folk, I'm on their side.
    And there I bide.

Obeo cruore fuso sine iure, sine lucro:
maris ora sancta semper tumulique erant Deo
sine martyris tuentis super aethera itinere.
Neque consecrata tractare ut ludibria licet
neque demovere: quae sunt generosa neque quatit
neque destruit perosus: vendi facile nequit
quod amas. Ad aequitatem et patrimonia morior,
violare quae nefas est. TAMEN HIC EGO MANEO.

– Itane mihi nominastis vexilla? Rideo:
minime gravabor, etsi sat ineptus erat honor.
Aliquantulum iuvari si Dorsetia potest,
patriam genusque signent. IBI ME FORE VOVEO.

GOLD, RED AND SILVER: THE DORSET FLAG

The gold of Dorset is the land
and all the folk who stood or stand
to treasure in their minds and bless
this tree, this field, this bell-peal heard
far off, this song or flight of bird,
this fresh stream filled with watercress.

Then Dorset's red is sober pride
and fortitude of hearts when tried,
the glow of cheeks at honest work
and honest play, the jests that tease
twixt friends completely at their ease,
the care for kin that none will shirk.

Amid these Dorset lays to view
a mark of even brighter hue,
untainted, incandescent, raw,
relentless like a silver wave
that dares the earth-born soul to brave
some sea of mystery and awe.

DORSETIAE
VEXILLUM

Aurum Dorsetiae terra est omnesque perenni
    tempore qui steterint
mente velut gaza posituri sanctum et amatum:
    aera sonora procul,

hic arbusta et agros, lapsum volucrisve canorem,
    plenum holus amne recens:
Dorsetiaeque rubrum virtus est casta rutique
    cordis inermis opes,

ludis atque labore genarum fervor honestus,
    grandis amicitiae
more licente ioci consanguineisque fidelis
    officio pietas:

at signum medio vexillo clarius istis
    Dorsetiane vides
tam purum candens quam saecula cuncta recusans
    pendere flaccum et iners,

per quod in aequor edax argentea pellicit unda
    terrigenas timidos
oceanumve pavoris ob alta arcana vocamur
    vincere Eleutheriae.

Morning song

How the sky now in the morning in beauty
outdoes friendly countryside and Proteus'
glistening threshold! Let Jupiter's handmaid
confess her obvious and silly theft,
who when she'd long neglected to sweep
dulled heaven, to rub it and make it fine

and coat it in gold, morosely hiding
away from the sun, jumped suddenly up
from her grieving languor with envy, intent
on abducting beauties that were not hers:
up aloft absurd Aurora made claim
to blue eyes and rose cheeks, though everyone knows

in that place that the colours belong to another –
that it's your charm that's being displayed.
That I might live in the heaven of the face
that I love and rejoicing in hunger touch
with these lips, O beautiful realm, the silken
straw of your hair, or lick, burnt up

with blessed thirst, thin dew from your
smooth brow! But there's no way into clouds
or air; longing's futile. I thought of how
in due order morning turns into noon,
noon into evening, evening into night.
That hours en masse one by one betray us

we never say. Spring, summer, autumn and winter
take turns; months follow each other. Over
short periods the year appears inconstant,
over long ages persistent. You likewise
fittingly show obedience to nature and
to yourself, transcending fraud and faith.

CARMEN MATUTINUM

Quam nunc mane polus specie rus vincit amicum
    micansque limen Protei!
Serva Iovis furtum fateatur apertum et inane,
    quae cum neglexerat diu
verrere hebes caelum, terere, ornare, integere auro,
    morosa soli condita,

prosiluit subito de languore invida tristi
    auferre honores exteros:
lumina caerulea et roseas Aurora superne
    insulsa praetendit genas,
quamquam ibidem sciat esse alienos quisque colores,
    tuam venustatem geri.

Ut possim caelo faciei vivere amatae
    et esuritione ovans
palpare his labiis, regio formosa, tuarum
    stramen comarum sericum
aut tenuem rorem de levi fronte perustus
    siti beata lambere!

Est tamen in nubes aditus vel in aëra nullus,
    desiderare futtile.
Quomodo fit memini matutinum ordine tempus
    meridies, meridies
vesper, vesper nox: nequaquam dicimus horas
    nos fallere omnes singulas:

ver, aestas vertunt autumnus hiemsque vicissim:
    menses sequuntur invicem:
fingitur inconstans spatiis brevioribus annus,
    aetate longa pervicax.
Naturae sic tu tibimetque decenter oboedis:
    fraudem fidemque praeteris.

Song of a Visitor to Athens

The North Wind stirs the yellowing leaf and soon
will send it with slapdash greed to soak in the mud:
My life too is touched by autumn, for now
white hairs are being scattered day by day.

You who died no older than I am, used you not
to dream, good Flaccus, of virgin Minerva's Acropolis
and the Propylaea and the Hill of Mars and the city
of learning to which young men come streaming together?

If I wish I can visit Oxford tomorrow, the proud
high point of my unpolished youth; but you
a god forbade to return to the Athens of renown,
given over to talk with its Stoa and Lyceum.

Let me be your eyes, your mind, let your tongue taste
in my mouth, with you let me wander eternal paths;
what you learnt then let me learn simply by drawing
breath among ruins and the warfare of the traffic.

Let the long spell of hot weather lengthen the joys of youth;
in an October hour who'd not want to linger here
beneath olive-trees, here where branches burdened
with fruit shade the hospitable bench of a simple tavern?

Let it be called by the name of Thespis from a nearby street;
let an orange-haired cat affectionately greet you, the noise
be silent, a single bird sing; you would think this was
the countryside; let wholesome resin flavour the wine,

squid or swordfish provide your meal. I suspect it was here,
away from lectures, that you imbibed truths; with insight
something wiser than Epicurus here imbued you;
here was vouchsafed a sense of eternal beauty.

CARMEN ATHENIS PEREGRINATI

Flavescens folium Boreas movet aureumque mittet
    praeceps avarus mox luto madere:
tangit et Autumnus vitam mihi, namque dissipantur
    canae comae iam singulis diebus.

Vivo non senior me mortue, nonne somniabas,
    honeste Flacce, virginis Minervae
Acropolin grandem Propylaeaque Martiumque Collem
    doctamque pubis confluentis urbem?

Oxonium potero cras visere si volam, superbum
    meae iuventae culmen impolitae:
te revenire deus vetuit tamen inclitas Athenas
    Stoa loquaces rite cum Lyceo.

Lumina sim tua, mens tua sim, tua lingua gustet ore:
    tecum pererrem semitas perennes:
quod didicisti tunc discam modo naribus reductum
    inter ruinas curruumque bellum.

Gaudia longa calor iuvenilia traxerit moratus:
    Octobris hora quis manere nolit
hic sub olivis, hic ubi pomifer hospitale ramus
    umbret sedile simplicis tabernae?

Thespidos appellent hanc nomine de via propinqua:
    te rufa feles suaviter salutet:
hic stridor sileat: volucris canat una: rus putares:
    resina vinum condiat salubris:

sepia vel xiphias det prandia. Suspicor remotum
    hic a cathedris te bibisse vera:
hic Epicuro te sapientius imbuit sapore:
    hic sempiterna est sensa pulchritudo.

PROLOGUE TO A STORY OF ALICE

Borne by the hours across the top of its journey
the sun gives a wash of gold to fields and trees.
In our boat we glide forth slowly, for they are little
and inexperienced arms that ply the oars
and in vain a little hand on the tiller tries
to hold course for those astray. Alas, three females
devoid of mercy, asking stories of one

in lazy dreams brought on by the heat unable
to move the lightest of feathers with his breath!
But will a lonely and feeble voice defeat
three tongues allied in hostile strategy?
Prima with thunderous flash commands a start,
more gently Secunda asks that there be humour,
and urgently Tertia breaks in extremely often;

yet suddenly silence overcomes them while
they follow in their minds an imagined girl
through settings prodigiously replete with wonders,
with bird and beast conversing pleasantly.
And not all the details strike the three as false
whose prolonged outpouring seems for a while
about to run dry the fount of images.

Exhausted and yearning languidly for rest
the narrator says "More of this later on." "The time
is now!" they then shout back in gleeful tone.
With the happenings of Wonderland invented
piece by piece, the story's gradually grown,
and when it's over home we then return,
happy sailors under the setting sun.

Provectus horis trans itineris verticem
illustrat auro sol agros et arbores.
Nos lintre lente labimur, nam bracchia
parum perita parva tractant palmulas
clavoque frustra parva manus errantibus
cursum tenere tentat. Heu clementia
tres destitutae, quae rogastis fabulas

segnis caloris impotentem somniis
movere plumam spiritu levissimam!
Num superet autem sola vox ac debilis
linguas coactas tres in hostilem modum?
Iubet tonante Prima initium fulmine,
petit Secunda mollius facetias,
persaepe et interfatur urgens Tertia:

tamen repente vincit has silentium
quae consequuntur mente fictam virginem
per loca repleta prodige miraculis,
avi loquente bestiaque comiter.
Nec omnia illis sentiuntur fallere
quorum parumper fusio productior
videtur exhaustura fontem imaginum.

Fessus quietem languide desiderans
narrator "olim cetera" inquit. "Hic adest
tempus" reclamant inde festivo sono.
Terrae novatis singulis Mirabilis
eventibus sic tarda crevit fabula,
qua terminata tunc remigramus domum
sub occidente sole laeti navitae.

Take, Alice, a tale designed for the young to hear
and lay it gently, I beg you, in the place
where girls entwine their memories' resources
into mystic garlands of joys from days gone by,
not unlike the flowers, now just a withered wreath,
which in faraway lands a traveller piously picked
when he had reached the shrine of a deity.

Narrationem liberis idoneam
Alicia sumptam pone leniter precor
ligant puellae qua memoriae copias
in gaudiorum serta veterum mystica,
similia florum iam coronae marcidae
quos in remotis tractibus carpsit pie
nactus viator numinis sacrarium.

THE WASP'S SONG

by Lewis Carroll

When I was young, my ringlets waved
And curled and crinkled on my head:
And then they said "You should be shaved,
And wear a yellow wig instead."

But when I followed their advice,
And they had noticed the effect
They said I did not look so nice
As they had ventured to expect.

They said it did not fit, and so
It made me look extremely plain:
But what was I to do, you know?
My ringlets would not grow again.

So now that I am old and grey,
And all my hair is nearly gone,
They take my wig from me and say
"How can you put such rubbish on?"

And still, whenever I appear,
They hoot at me and call me "Pig!"
And that is why they do it, dear,
Because I wear a yellow wig.

VESPAE CARMEN

Iuveni crispis capite ante mihi
cirri cumulis agitabantur:
tunc "decet" aiunt "tondere comas,
gerere et flavum deinde galerum."

Sum consilium rite secutus:
animadverso tamen effectu
me pulchellum dixere minus
quam spe dubia fore duxissent

subque galero male dimenso
ferre egregie foedam faciem.
Quid dic agerem? Crescere cirri
similes iterum non saepe solent.

Cum canities paeneque plenum
mihi calvitium cecidere seni,
ecce galerum vertice demunt
"audes gerere haec scruta?" rogantes.

Me nunc etiam si forte vident
ludificantur vocitantque suem:
unica causa est inimicitiae
flavum, virgo cara, galerum!

The State of Happiness
Paraphrase of a School Song

The state of happiness is born from truth;
Telemachus, let those desiring joy
seek what is true; thus shall the dominie
in school exhort with ardour, this behest
the scholar vigilantly shall obey.
Freude vom Wahren be your rule of life;
come, always how, why, what take care to learn;
questioning wisely sets your spirit free
and knowledge soon to shine forth cheers your soul.
The slothful pass their days in tedium,
while due achievement earns the diligent
years of felicity; toil at the quest
for understanding; this will in the end
bring you delight; make this precept your own.

Magpies

To English bird-diviners one means sorrow,
two magpies joy, a daughter three, but four
a son; such birds still walk Askrikegatan,
to me your street for ever and most fair.
Woe! On the playing fields, in Tessin Park
and on this street one magpie at a time
is all I see; must I sad-omened now
be sad? Heaven has no time; perhaps already
we're feres, each love I've ever loved and I.
Who'll tell what could (oh joy!) be done or had
not here but there perhaps, where laws and limits
of earth and earthly beings lose their strength?

De Veritate Nascitur Felicitas
Carminis Scholastici Paraphrasis Latina

De veritate nascitur felicitas:
gaudia qui cupiunt, Telemache, verum postulent:
    hortetur ardens haec magister in schola
discipulusque vigil praescriptioni pareat.

    Chara ex alethou norma vitae sit tibi:
quomodo, cur, age, quid in omne cures discere:
    docte rogando liberatur spiritus
atque hilarant animam elucituri nuntii.

    Dies teruntur a pigris in taedio,
dat tamen adsiduis annos beatos dignum opus:
    labore consectare tu scientiam:
laetificatus eris: hoc redde praeceptum tuum.

Picae

Triste omen pica una duaeque hilare, omina natae
tres, nati tamen auspicibus sunt quattuor Anglis:
inque Via spatiantur aves tales etiam nunc
Ascricae mihi quae tua erit pulcherrima semper.
Singula vae video tantum exemplaria picae
ludorum in campis Tessinique illius Horto
inque via: iamne omina ero per tristia tristis?
Tempore eget caelum: comites fortasse sumus iam
quisque meus quocumque die dilectus eroton
atque ego. Quis ferret quid io facile aut habile esset,
haud hic sed fortasse illic ubi iura modique
terrae terrestrisque animantis robur omittunt?

I Have Sinned

I have sinned: nonetheless as usual golden Phoebus
is still there in the heavens. Fortune has prevented
the mass of my sins from affecting the sun, the sky,
the green earth, the sea, the mountains, the stars, the moon.
Fortune, hope of the sinner and rescue of wrongdoers,
it is right to thank you who govern all destinies well.

The Poet Dejected

The best that asweat in your rôle as bard you might cobble together
would be chance slips of the pen to the eyes – well, the ears – of Venus
given to sweetness of speech or Apollo mighty in art
or the Muses chaste in style or Minerva replete with learning:
for we are chance slips of the bed and falling informs our uprising.

The Sundew

When first you are confronted with a sundew,
you may conclude we tend to place an undue
reliance on soft plants not eating creatures,
one of their rather prepossessing features.
But Nature's gifts are free; she'll not refund you.

Peccavi

Peccavi. Nihilo minus aureus ut solet exstat
in caelo Phoebus: vetuit Fortuna meorum
vim peccatorum solem contingere, caelum,
tellurem viridem, mare, montes, sidera, lunam.
Spes tibi peccantis Fortuna salusque malorum
fas agere est grates bene quae regis omnia fata.

Poëta Maestus

Optima quae sudore queas componere vates
sint calami lapsus oculis aut auribus usae
blanditiis Veneris vel Apollinis arte potentis
castarumve Camenarum doctaeve Minervae:
nam lapsus thalami sumus exortique labantes.

Drosera

Aspiciens primum Droseram nos ducere posses
credere plus aequo teneris animalia plantis
non comedi, quod proprietas sit amoenior harum.
Non tamen hoc gratis quae dat Natura rependet.

Sweet Williams

The flowers have been stripped of their comrades
and either one has been stripped of his friend;
one roams the streets weighed down with love,
while the other is held in that prison they call
an asylum, and the pair of Sweet Williams grieves
at being deprived of its very self.

An Old Man's Wisdom

Hear wisdom told
by one who's reached the age that's old:
others are less
like you than you could ever guess.

A Rare Bird

Birds of a common feather
they say will flock together.
Why am just I, Dame Luck,
this strange, this lone lame duck?

To Someone Getting Old

The more death the loathsome neglects you and yields you longevity,
the more you will find yourself anguishing over life's brevity.

Dianthi Barbati

Nudati flores sociis et uterque sodali:
    unus per plateas errat amore gravis,
alterum habet carcer tamen ille vocatus asylum:
    parque Dianthorum se sibi deesse dolet.

Senis Sapientia

Ecce senectutem nacti sapientia dicta:
esse minus similes alios tibi quam fore credas.

Rara Avis

Convolaturas colorum similium dicunt aves.
Cur modo ego sum rara, sola, Domina Fors, haec clauda anas?

Ad Senescentem

Quo longaevus eris magis invisoque neglectus
funere eo brevitate magis vexabere vitae.

To His Dictionary (Lewis and Short)

You *levis* – light – and short? That's wrong:
you're heavy and distinctly long.
Scholars are not by you misled
except when these two names are read.

To Truth: A Hymn for Europe

Truth,
Leader and Servant,
Torch for our path and Light for our minds!
To You our continent shall be dedicated
and each one of us shall give his heart.
The culture to which You reveal Yourself
Europe's vitality shall maintain.
I ask of You that by Your nurturing
the potential of every citizen
shall bear fruit.

Ad Dictionarium Suum

Num Levis et Brevis es? Potius gravis ac bene longus.
Non nisi nominibus studiosos decipis istis.

Εἰς τὴν Ἀλήθειαν Ὕμνος Εὐρωπαῖος
(Ad Veritatem Hymnus Europaeus)

Veritas, dux et ministra, fax viae, lux mentibus,
continens tibi dicetur detque quisque cor suum:
cui pates humanitatem curet Europae vigor:
indoli cuiusque civis te rogo fructus colas.

Vel consuetudini cantorum hodiernorum aptatus:

Veritas, dux et ministra, fax viae, lux mentium,
continens tibi dicetur detque quisque cor suum:
cui pates humanitatem curet Europae vigor:
indoli cuiusque civis tu colas fructus precor.

Selected Epigrams

on some of the classes that have left
ST. CATHERINE'S SCHOOL in Uppsala

The OX ploughs up fields of study and meadows of discourse;
  the OX turns everything over, the certain, the presumed, the holy.

Not taken into servitude, the DEER is the lord of the park;
  with unflagging zeal it polishes its beautiful horns.

Who knows what murky path the CAT takes between open places
                                                    and halls?
  Where does it suddenly come from? Where does it quietly go?

GRIFFIN, wise yet playful, lazy yet bold, actor and originator,
  a noble hybrid you were, all things to all men you will be.

Young and high-flying the SWALLOW dislikes the barns
  and the inhabitable, honest earth of human beings;
  but when it is fully grown it will gather clay.

The dripping IBIS keeps company with its fellows in the swamp,
  shakes its wings, splashes, screeches and hops in the water.

The LION fights and plays and roars and is silent;
  he who sees it has no doubt that it rules the plains.

The OWL showed itself so wise that Minerva herself
  for her emblem chose this venerable bird.

Graceful GAZELLE dwelling among crags, you conduct yourself
  even-temperedly before our eyes and bring joy to our hearts.

The PHOENIX continually arises before us with the sun and is reborn;
  it can hardly remember the egg or the fact that a day has passed.

RHINOCEROS with your thick skin, wrathful and rebellious,
  having been gored oh how I would like to have your hide!

This is how the SALAMANDER conquers death in fire:
  by not getting hot; with its mind it freezes its innards.

Epigrammata Scholastica Selecta

super classibus quibusdam quae discesserunt a
SCHOLA SANCTAE CATHARINAE Upsalensi

BOS obarat campos studiorum et prata loquelae:
omnia BOS vertit, certa, putata, sacra.

CERVUS non capitur servus: dominatur in horto:
perpetuo studio cornua pulchra polit.

FELIS iter quis scit tenebrosum inter fora et aulas?
Unde venit subito? Quo taciturna redit?

GRYPS sapiens lusor, piger, audax, comicus, auctor,
nobilis hibrida eras: omnibus omnia eris.

Horrea humumque habitabilem honestam hominum horret
HIRUNDO
iunior altivolans: sed lutum adulta leget.

IBIS cum paribus se congregat uda palude,
alam agitat, strepitat, stridet aquisque salit.

Luctantur luduntque frementque silentque LEONES:
qui videt haud dubitat quin loca plana regant.

NOCTUA tam prudens exstabat ut ipsa Minerva
optaret signis hanc venerabilem avem.

O qui pulcher ORYX colis aspera te geris aequo
ante oculos habitu cordaque laeta creas.

PHOENIX perpetuo cum sole novatur obortus:
vix ovi meminit nec periisse diem.

RHINOCEROS spissae pellis truculente rebellis,
o vellem pellem punctus habere tuam!

Sic superat SALAMANDRA periclum mortis in igne:
haud nimis ardendo: viscera mente gelat.

The nicely-hued, murmuring TURTLE-DOVE rejects the bran
and picks from the ground the finest grains of understanding.

Wisdom leads the SWORDFISH through the colonnades
of the gymnasion under the water; they glide
hither and thither; to their eyes everything is transparent.

The astonishing WHALES have explored the depth of the ocean,
kept unharmed by a rule of inviolate calm.

The CENTAURS, uniting the forms of men and horses,
are strong with the robustness and power of both body and mind.

It likes everything that is and understands everything that is,
the fortune-bringing DOLPHIN, intelligent and pleasant.

Nothing leaves the memory of the ELEPHANTS; may the good
provide them with strength and the bad with forewarning.

Under its helmet-crest the COCKEREL pierces us with an angry eye,
aware of the wonderful riches of its empire.

The pitiful, recalcitrant KID is to be sacrificed on the altar of learning;
it is unwilling, but through the might of its elders it will be willing.

Our industrious flock of WOLVES keeps silence towards the Moon,
loving rather the subtle light of Pallas Athene.

The musical voice of the BLACKBIRD beautifully mixes low tones
with high;
its beak is splendid with gold and its sable wings mourn.

The NAUTILUS, contemplating the deepest secrets of the sea,
neither strays towards the waves above nor flies among the birds.

In turn the WILD ASS runs to meet us and flees away from us,
first impossible to tame but later ready to be led.

They say TIGERS never lose their stripes; and those that have
been tamed will not lack the marks the school has provided.

TURTURE purpureo cum murmure furfure iacto
optima consilii grana leguntur humo.

Xystis submersis XIPHIAS sapientia ducit:
huc illuc fluitant: omne liquere vident.

BALAENAE mirae pelagi novere profundum
quas regit incolumes non vitiata quies.

CENTAURI iunctis hominum formis et equorum
corporis atque animi robore vique valent.

Diligit omne quod est quodque est intellegit omne
faustus DELPHINUS callidus atque placens.

Ex ELEPHANTORUM nil mentibus emigrat unquam:
confirmetque bonum praemoneatque malum.

GALLUS sub galea penetrat nos lumine saevo:
imperii proprii mirificas scit opes.

HAEDUS oblatus erit miser atque invitus in ara
doctrinae: non vult: vi seniore volet.

Lunam nostra silet studiosa caterva LUPORUM:
Palladis haec potius subtile lumen amat.

Musica vox MERULAE pulchre grave miscet acuto:
rostrum auro splendet luget et ala nigra.

NAUTILUS ima maris meditans arcana neque errat
ad superas undas nec volat inter aves.

Occurrit nobis ONAGER refugitque vicissim,
indocilis primum, deinde paratus agi.

TIGRES dicuntur non unquam perdere virgas:
nec deerunt domitis quae schola signa tulit.

The FOXES are leaving the countryside to seek their sustinence
    in the city: it is an alma mater, a nourishing mother,
    that makes the cunning creatures healthy and sleek.

You fall to the earth and cannot get up again? ELK, you disprove
    the stories; you often get up from the ground.

The beast may have a large body and an enormous head,
    but you, our BISON, possess a mighty heart and brain.

Up to now the SWAN sings often and gladly without coming to harm;
    throughout its life may it be mindful of the end
    and yet sing wherever it may be.

Like a fawn you flee from me, FALLOW-DEER, but there will be,
                                   FALLOW-DEER,
    another master by whom you may be calmed.

The DORMOUSE whom the ancients liked to eat with honey
    now enjoys the sweet poetry of an ancient bard.

Mindlessly flicking the seaweed with its fins the GOLDFISH
    does seem made of gold; precious it is to us in the water.

Unless it is you, hard MUREX, that dye the soft cloth, its splendour
    is not increased by a sun that tends to put beauty to flight.

Playing with claws retracted amuses the young PANTHERS;
    but often enough they fight with both claw and tooth.

GOLDCREST, little bird, you used to lack the crown that you now
    show off, being worthy of your new mark of distinction.

The WASP flies whither it will, be the journey long or short;
    with confidence in its sting it can provide its own stimulation.

VULPES rus linquunt epulas ut in urbe requirant:
mater in urbe vafras alma nitere facit.

Accidis ad terram non surrectura? Refellis
historias ALCES: saepe resurgis humo.

Bestia si magnum corpus gerat et caput ingens,
cor cerebrumque BISON grandia noster habes.

CYGNUS saepe libenter adhuc canit ac sine damno:
per vitam memoret finem at ubique canat.

Defugis hinnuleo similis me, DAMMA, sed alter
qui reddat placidam, DAMMA, magister erit.

GLIRI quem veteres cum melle libenter edebant
vatis nunc veteris dulce poëma placet.

HIPPURUS pinnis algas sine mente flagellans
aureus aspicitur: carus habetur aquis.

MUREX tu nisi dure coloras textile molle
splendidius non fit sole fugante decus.

PANTHERAS iuvenes ludus iuvat ungue retracto:
certant ungue tamen denteque saepe satis.

REGULE parva volucris egebas ante corona
quam nunc ostentas dignus honore novo.

VESPA volat quo vult, via si sit longa brevisve:
confidens stimulo se stimulare valet.

Haikus Translated

Version of a Japanese haiku

Ages of dew
are eras of dew, but ah,
and yet and yet!

Change

Flee change;
there are tears for
new things.

A Portuguese proverb

A cat bitten by
a snake as a kitten will
thenceforth fear a rope.

About himself

I have found
on earth no companion
and no leader.

After reading a certain poem of Horace

Did Pyrrha, simple
in her neatness, want
to hear the poem?

Haicua

Versio haicus Iaponici

Sunt roris aeva
saecula roris, at heu
tamen tamenque!

Mutatio

Mutationem
aufuge: sunt lacrimae
rerum novarum.

Proverbium Lusitanicum

Feles ab angui
parvula morsa dehinc
funem timebit.

De se ipso

Tellure nullum
repperimus comitem
ducemque nullum.

Carmine quodam Horatii lecto

Num Pyrrha simplex
munditiis voluit
audire carmen?

Again after reading a poem of Horace

The days are tedious.
Bitter winter is on its last legs – what
is holding up the spring?

Thickets

Dense and
impenetrable thickets,
human hearts.

Saltsjöbaden 5 May 2011

The silver of the water
shines more white than the silent
cloud above.

9 May 2011

Summer brings guilt,
winter anger. When shall I be
able to be happy?

Another Haiku 9 May 2011

Having once forgotten
I remember: O that forgetfulness
might be at hand!

Item carmine Horatii lecto

Taedet dierum.
Solvitur acris hiems –
quid ver retardat?

Virgulta

Virgulta densa
impenetrabilia,
humana corda.

Natabuli Maris Salsi die V Maii MMXI

Argentum aquarum
candidius supera
silente nube.

Die IX Maii MMXI

Culpam dat aestas,
iram et hiems. Potero
gaudere quando?

Item die IX Maii MMXI

Oblitus olim
sum memor: o utinam
oblivia adsint!

22 May 2011

Manly verse
thrashes the words so that they
may be strong and fly.

9 October 2011

Reject equality:
it is ordained that human beings
may not be compared.

Another Haiku 9 October 2011

Dreams disgust,
for they ask and yet are not
asked themselves.

12 October 2011

Autumn the time of
year when spring can
best be appraised.

19 October 2011

At night each
foot can see and settles
in its own slipper.

Die XXII Maii MMXI

Versus virilis
verberat ut valeant
volentque verba.

Die IX Octobris MMXI

Aequalitatem
reice: fas homines
non comparari.

Item die IX Octobris MMXI

Fastidiuntur
somnia, namque rogant
at non rogantur.

Die XII Octobris MMXI

Autumnus anni
tempus ubi melius
ver aestimetur.

Die XIX Octobris MMXI

Uterque noctu
pes videt ac solea
sua residet.

Three Songs in Mediaeval Style

Feast Day Song for Saint Catherine

Praise be to you, O Lord!
Praise be to you, O Lord!

I should not like Saint Catherine
to be forgotten,
the heroine of the school
who flourished long ago,
her wise understanding,
her educated mind,
her beautiful countenance,
a flower of youth.

Praise be to you, O Lord!
Praise be to you, O Lord!

When a king desired her
she demurred,
proclaiming faith in Christ
to the unhappy sinner;
he sent fifty men to her,
men out of the ordinary,
but they were powerless
to persuade the virgin.

Praise be to you, O Lord!
Praise be to you, O Lord!

CARMINA STILO MEDIAEVALI CONFECTA

Cantus Festivus de Sancta Catharina

Δόξα Σοι, Κύριε!
Δόξα Σοι, Κύριε!

Sanctam Catharinam,
scholae heroinam
quae florebat olim
ignorari nolim,
sensum sapientem,
eruditam mentem,
faciem formosam,
iuventutis rosam.

Δόξα Σοι, Κύριε!
Δόξα Σοι, Κύριε!

Rex cum cupiebat
illa abnuebat,
clamans fidem Christi
peccatori tristi:
misit ille viros
quinquaginta miros,
impotentes vere
virgini suadere.

Δόξα Σοι, Κύριε!
Δόξα Σοι, Κύριε!

She was fixed to a wheel
of hitherto unknown kind;
the wheel being soon destroyed,
she remained unmarried.
Mightily irritated
the angry king ordered
the head of the faithful flower
to be severed by the sword.

Praise be to you, O Lord!
Praise be to you, O Lord!

To a mountain beyond
the horizon angels
carried the lamented
and hallowed body.
Prepare a path for us,
make it clear by your example,
turn it heavenwards,
holy Catherine!

Praise be to you, O Lord!
Praise be to you, O Lord!

Fixa est in rotam
antehac ignotam;
rota mox dirupta,
perrexit innupta;
valde inritatus
iussit rex iratus
caput floris fidi
gladio abscidi.

Δόξα Σοι, Κύριε!
Δόξα Σοι, Κύριε!

Angeli ad montem
praeter horizontem
portaverunt planctum
corpus sacrosanctum.
Viam nobis para,
exemplo declara,
ad caelos inclina,
sancta Catharina.

Δόξα Σοι, Κύριε!
Δόξα Σοι, Κύριε!

A Birthday Song for the Saviour
in which the earth is compared to the Grail

Our cold, dark earth has been chosen
to be filled with the mixture of blood
and water that flowed abundantly
from the side of the wounded Son.
The Father wishes to shatter the separation
between the heavenly and the earthly:
the earth that had abused the betrothal
shall become His daughter-in-law.
    Blessed is he who comes
    in the Lord's name.
    Hosanna in the highest!
    You shall be the Milk
    and Honey of the lands,
    our heavenly Way born
    of Mary! O Truth, O Life
    united with the stock
    of Joachim and Anna!
    Hosanna, hosanna!

Eve, Adam's rib and wife, remains
the stem of our uncivilized people;
now the bud of the eternal Lord
is grafted on to a virgin twig;
rough blight is smoothed away;
the sap of spring moistens dry bones.

The exhausted soil was sleeping;
then a prophet sang of the morning star;
the Sun of Righteousness proclaims day;
dew is distilled, destroying fever;
as Rachel perished giving birth,
now Mary as mother conquers death.

Carmen Natalicium Salvatoris
in quo mundus illi "Gradali" illustri confertur

Nostra tellus frigida obscura
lecta est quam impleat mixtura
sanguinis et aquae large fusa
ex afflicto Nati latere.
Pater vult discrimen quatere:
nurus fit sponsalibus abusa.
    Benedictus qui
      venit in nomine Domini.
    Hosanna in excelsis!
    Terrarum Lac et Mel sis,
    caelestis nostra Via
    quam peperit Maria!
    O Veritas, o Vita
    cum genere unita
    de Ioachim et Anna!
    Hosanna, hosanna!

Heva, costa Adae ac marita,
restat gentis durae stirps avita:
nunc in virgam virginem aeterni
germen Domini inseritur:
scabra sic robigo teritur:
ossa sicca rigant succi verni.
    Benedictus...

Somniabant sola obsoleta,
cecinit luciferum propheta:
diem Sol Iustitiae indicit:
ros stillatur febrem feriens:
cum Rachel pariret periens,
iam Maria mater mortem vicit.
    Benedictus...

O first-fruits, O true vine, we orphans shall
be gently raised by you and and made productive,
we who bound and pruned you to provide
everyday life with a sovereign remedy;
you grant wine to the feast at Cana;
"amen" is transmuted into consolation.

Shining White
Verses on a Dorset holy woman

Shining white, O holy martyr
of Christ, you grew up destined
to die at the hands of evil men,
to enter the choir of celestial beings:
and even more shining white you receive,
like the topmost stone of a temple,
full rewards in heaven: I wish
to be raised up by your prayers!

O primitiae, o vera vitis,
orbos nos fecundans colas mitis
qui te resecuimus ligatum
ut sit panacea trivio:
Canae vinum das convivio:
in solamen est "amen" mutatum.
    Benedictus...

Candida Crevisti
Versus de sancta muliere Dorsetiana

Candida crevisti,
martyr sancta Christi,
manibus moritura malorum,
ingressura caelestium chorum:
candidiorque capis,
ut summus templi lapis,
praemia plena polo:
precibus tolli volo!

Afterword

The poetry of recent times is many-faceted in a way the ancient and mediaeval worlds could not have contemplated. To write in Latin nowadays cannot mean cutting oneself off, if that were possible, from the culture in which we live – and no decision on how we wish to write can separate us from our literary culture, so great is the liberty it grants us.

I prefer to work in quantitative metres, i.e. in rhythmic patterns of long and short syllables. When I read Horace's odes and epodes the charm of the varying rhythms is as essential to my enjoyment as the concepts denoted by the words forming the patterns. Taking my cue from him, or rather, I suppose, his Greek predecessors, and aware of novelties introduced in late antiquity and during the renaissance,[1] I have invented a number of pleasing and well-balanced strophic structures of my own.

Whatever language, style or metre one writes in, genuine poetry must, I am convinced, emerge from the whole personality, the head and the heart together.

The British habit in recent centuries has been unreflectingly to treat the writing of Latin verse as necessarily a question of close imitation or parody. In Horace the Minstrel (Kineton 1969) Noel A. Bonavia-Hunt rails against inadequate attention to ancient models on the part of some learned versifiers of the recent past and provides detailed statistics of Horace's actual practice (word disposition in relation to feet, the placing of the caesura, the prevalence of long final syllables and so on) in each single type of verse. At the same time he constantly claims, but fails to show with reasoned discussion, the aesthetic benefit of such an approach. Whatever the educational worth of such verse-writing its priorities are not compatible those of a genuine poet.

---

1 E.g. for late antiquity Ausonius IV xvii; IV xxviii and XIX lxxxix; V x; Boethius *De Consolatione Philosophiae, passim*; Prudentius the *Praefatio* (*Per quinquennia iam decem*) and elsewhere his frequent use of various types of verse in strophes of three, four or five. For a renaissance example see Paul Melissus' (1539–1602) ungainly alternating hexameters and Alcaic hendecasyllabics under the heading Venusia (Eckart Schäfer, *Deutscher Horaz*, Wiesbaden 1976 page 72).

In fact its educational validity must be called into question by another consideration. There is a great risk that shallow, intellectually and emotionally undemanding mimicry will be harmful to the development of taste and sensitivity when there is contact with real poetry.

At worst pupils and undergraduates may be expected to produce Latin hexameters or elegiacs that do not only regurgitate an existing piece of writing – usually English rhyming verse – but also keep the same number of lines: this I call the Procrustes' bed school of translation, as it generally involves stretching out snatches of the original so as to fill the Latin metrical model, thus attenuating their impact. Mythological name-dropping, however incongruous, will be encouraged, as will the hijacking of actual quotations from classical sources.

Let us see what the British approach involves in practice by examining a mere pair of lines, picked out at random, as treated by J. F. Crace, a master at Eton, in Some Latin Verses, Cambridge 1935, a little book intended to edify pupils and interest colleagues. On pages 22, 23:

> Go, feeble tyrant, and in vain
> Thy fruitless conquest boast ...   (Anon.)

> I nunc et jacta vanus victricia frustra
> arma, levesque istas perde, tyranne, minas.   (Crace's elegiacs)

Go now and boast emptily of (your) unavailingly victorious weapons, and be rid, tyrant, of those lightweight menaces of yours.

As one might predict the need to expand content has the effect of weakening and blurring. "Feeble tyrant", which in order to impress needs to come in all its succinctness near the beginning of the passage, has been delayed and insipidly spun out into a separate clause. In a school exercise to come up with Virgil's *victricia arma* would be sure to win brownie points, but "unavailingly victorious weapons" is pompously inept. What Crace found meritorious is in reality rather a botched job. Any concise and straightforward rendering is preferable. In (Horatian) iambic trimeter for instance:

Abi tyranne debilis, victoria
nihil ferente gloriare inaniter ...

Dactylic rhythms go equally well. My offering might open a set of hexameters:

Cede tyranne parum fortis frustraque triumpho
te sterili iacta ...

It would also fit elegiacs were it not that the leanness of the English lines cannot be matched to the discrete, well-rounded distichs which the elegiac genre requires.

What I have called the British approach has its partial antithesis in some other recent Latin verse, where it is an attitude of *laissez-faire* regarding prosody that finds its match in an easy-going banality of ideas.

The exigencies of metre are important not only because of the satisfying auditory result but also because the attention a poet lavishes on them can help him to come to a purified and deepened understanding of the essence of what is to be expressed. In Tradition and Originality in Roman Poetry Gordon Williams writes (on page 787) "the increase of technical difficulty has, up to a point, an enabling effect on the poetic imagination". This can be compared with John Dryden's views on rhyme as declared in his lengthy dedication of The Rival Ladies to the Earl of Orrery. He speaks of "an objection which some have made, that rhyme is only an embroidery of sense, to make that, which is ordinary in itself, pass for excellent with less examination." He continues, "But certainly, that which most regulates the fancy, and gives the judgment its busiest employment, is like to bring forth the richest and clearest thoughts."

Those who have learnt to appreciate Latin poetry have almost certainly done so through Horace and his contemporaries and successors. A poet must grasp with joy the requirement to please the taste of connoisseurs, who have the potential to gain most from his offerings.

This does not entail always playing safe. Our sophisticates must be supposed able to appreciate a risky dodge when it is artistically motivated. As Guy Lee asks in *Otium cum indignitate* (Quality and Pleasure in Latin Poetry, edited by Woodman and West, London 1974), "... are poets never to be allowed a *hapax legomenon* or a new combination of words?" But if outright mistakes of usage or metre should be discovered here the reader must blame them not on indifference but on lamentable inobservance. He is not begrudged the pleasure of correcting them.

In certain contexts a present-day author must be allowed to employ a few terms in their post-classical, Christian and mediaeval senses – *cor, spiritus, ecclesia, Creator, Salvator* etc. New coinages must be permitted, such as *laophorum* for bus, and also modern usages such as *pellicula* for film and *raeda* for motor vehicle.

Is it letting the side down to provide Latin poems with modern language counterparts (in this case of varying character) on their first appearance in print? In an ideal world it might be thought so, but there is no shame in being realistic.[2] The prospective readers who value a little support would seem far to outnumber those intent on taking their Latin neat.

Stephen Coombs

---

2   When Frédéric Mistral published his poems and verse narratives in Provençal he provided literal French prose translations; had he not done so, would he have been chosen to receive the Nobel Prize for Literature in 1904 jointly with José Echegaray? In 2007 Joseph Tusiani's collection of Latin poems In Nobis Caelum was presented to the public in the august Supplementa Humanistica Lovaniensia together with translations in Italian.

Notes on the Poems

Urbes – Cities

OLISIPO – LISBON: *fata* (fates) refer to the fados that have been sung in the city since the nineteenth century and still continue as a living and developing tradition.

OXONIUM – OXFORD: Isis is a name given to the Thames as it flows through Oxford.

Occasiones Servatae – Moments held

These poems comment upon photographs taken by the author some time ago, mainly in the 60s and 70s.

FINIS TERRAE GALLAECUS – GALICIAN FISTERRA/FINISTERRA: reference is made to Mozart's The Magic Flute.

Fragmenta Mythica – Seven Poems 1974–1979 (Mythic Fragments)

In this case the English poems are originals which the Latin verses paraphrase.

LAZARUS NUNC OPPERIENS – LAZARUS: the story of the raising of Lazarus from the dead is found in John xi 1–44.

Onyx Nardi – The Box of Balm

In the verses indicated in the following list references are made to poems of Horace, mostly to be found among the four books of the *Carmina* (C.), in English commonly called the Odes.

3 – C. IV xii	49 – C. IV iii 22
15 – C. IV xii 5–8	59 – C. I i 1, 2
33 – Epodes xiv 5, C. II xvii 1	63 – C. IV iii 16
41 – C. I i 36	74, 75 – C. IV xii 17, 21, 22
42 – C. III xxx 1	79 – C. I iii 8, 10
43 – C. II xx 12	85–88 – C. IV vii 25–28

This piece has its origin in the final scene of the author's play *Tidens Törst* (*The Thirst of Time*, cf. C. IV xii 13), performed in 2004 to celebrate the tenth anniversary of the founding of Katarinaskolan in

Uppsala. For *Ligurinus* as the name of a young friend of Horace see C. IV i and x.

When this poem was entered in the 2013 Certamen Scaevolae Mariotti (where it was awarded *magna laus*) the following *Argumentum* was provided: *Adseverat Ligurinus, adulescens amicus Quinti Horatii Flacci, se intellegere significationem cuiusdam carminis ab hoc auctore nuper editi iamque controversiae subiecti in quo poeta mortuus Vergilius vocari videtur. In explicationem Ligurinus interdum verba aliorum carminum Horatii citans exprimit asperitate aliquantum puerili notiones suas, quae tamen vi non carent. In fine dialogi Horatius respondet.* – Ligurinus, a young friend of Quintus Horatius Flaccus (i.e. Horace), maintains that he understands the meaning of a certain poem recently published by this author and already the subject of controversy. It seems to be addressed to the deceased poet Virgil. In explanation, and from time to time quoting from other poems of Horace, Ligurinus expresses his ideas with a somewhat puerile crudeness; they are however not without force. At the end of the dialogue Horace replies.

A jest coupling the two distinct functions of sweet-smelling balm, on the one hand to give pleasure to guests at parties and on the other to anoint the dead before burial, can be found in an epigram of Martial (III xii):

> *Unguentum fateor bonum dedisti*
> *convivis here, sed nihil scidisti.*
> *Res salsa est bene olere et esurire.*
> *Qui non cenat et unguitur Fabelle,*
> *hic vere mihi mortuus videtur.*

– I admit it was good unguent you provided for your guests yesterday, but you carved no meat. To smell nice but go hungry – there's a sauce! In truth, Fabellus, to me anyone who doesn't dine and gets anointed is like a dead person.

In connection with *oblectare* in the final verse dubious readers are referred to Birger Bergh, On Passive Imperatives in Latin, Acta Universitatis Upsaliensis, Studia Latina Upsaliensia 8, Uppsala 1975.

Mustela vel potius Telamus – The Weasel: or rather, Telamus

For *Telamus* as a river name W. Pape (*Handwörterbuch der griechischen Sprache*, Dritter Band *Wörterbuch der griechischen Eigennamen*, Braunschweig 1849) gives Τήλαμος, ό, *Fluß in Scythien*, Lycophr. 1333.

Otto Strandman, Swedish sculptor, 1871–1960.

Iambic trimeter acatalectic in four-line strophes.

Vox Ter Cupida – Thrice Yearning Voice

PUER – A BOY: cf. John vi 8–13; also Matt. vi 12; xxv 14, 15, 27; xxii 19–21; Gen. i 26, 27. Second Pythiambic metre (cf. Horace Epode xvi).

ADULESCENS – A YOUTH: cf. Mark xiv 51, 52. Alcaic strophe.

IUVENIS – A YOUNG MAN: cf. Mark xvi, 5–7. Third Archilochian metre (cf. Horace Epode ix).

Extemporalia ante Ver Inceptum – Pre-Spring Improvisations

DIURSOLMIAE – IN DJURSHOLM: In Epode xvi Horace speaks of Rome not having been destroyed by its various enemies, *nec fera caerulea domuit Germania pube*, "nor did savage Germania with its 'blue youth' tame (Rome)". The blueness of Germania's youth has usually been explained as referring to eye-colour or to the use of woad on the body. Gainsborough's painting The Blue Boy (ca. 1770) is in the Huntingdon Museum in California.

APUD LITUS SEPTENTRIONALE LACUS MAELARIS – ON THE NORTHERN BANK OF LAKE MÄLAREN: cf. II Cor. iii 6.

De Non Haesitante Amore – Unhesitating Love

Nox erat et caelo are the opening words of Horace's Epode xv.

Scaena Brahmsiana – Brahmsian Scene

The poem concerns an imaginary nineteenth century performance of Brahms's Rhapsody for contralto, men's chorus and orchestra op. 53, known as the Alto Rhapsody. Brahms's choice of text from

Goethe's *Harzreise im Winter,* paraphrased in four sections in the Latin poem, reads as follows:

> *Aber abseits wer ist's?*
> *Ins Gebüsch verliert sich sein Pfad,*
> *hinter ihm schlagen die Sträuche zusammen,*
> *das Gras steht wieder auf,*
> *die Öde verschlingt ihn.*

> *Ach, wer heilet die Schmerzen*
> *des, dem Balsam zu Gift wird?*
> *Der sich Menschenhaß*
> *aus der Fülle der Liebe trank?*
> *Erst verachtet, nun ein Verächter,*
> *zehrt er heimlich auf*
> *seinen eig'nen Wert*
> *in ung'nügender Selbstsucht.*

> *Ist auf deinem Psalter,*
> *Vater der Liebe,*
> *ein Ton seinem Ohre vernehmlich,*
> *so erquicke sein Herz!*
> *Öffne den umwölkten Blick*
> *über die tausend Quellen*
> *neben dem Durstenden*
> *in der Wüste.*

Velut Carmen Veritas – Truth as Poem

Serendip, i.e. Ceylon or Sri Lanka – the fairy-story The Three Princes of Serendip gave rise to the English expression "serendipity". The Dorchester of the poem is the county town of Dorset, England.

Simul Evidentia atque Obscura – Things at the Same Time both Plain and Obscure

An velut carmen and "Or could pure simple truth" are the opening words of the preceding poem Velut Carmen Veritas and its translation.

Ad Ingratos Datores – An undankbare Geber

The German text is the original and the Latin a paraphrase. Iambic trimeter acatalectic in four-line strophes.

Icon Sanctorum Flori et Lauri – The Icon of Saints Florus and Laurus

The Swedish verses of which this is a paraphrase were inspired by the decision of Katarinaskolan in Uppsala to present an icon of these saints to its principal initial benefactor:

De heliga Florus och Laurus Ikon

I (*till de heliga Florus och Laurus*)

Ni högg i sten. Det skulle bli ett tempel.
Men hjärtats slag i era fromma bröst
bar ekot av en slagen Herres röst,
som bjöd att motta korsets segerstämpel.

Urstenen mejslades. Urvärldens hedning
signades, formades, blev rörd till handling.
Templet och folket drogs in i förvandling.
Bygget och byn erkände Kristus ledning.

Ni greps och slängdes i en gammal brunn.
Brunnens tillslutning. Markernas förvildning.
Slut på uppbyggelse och slut på bildning:
men er bedrift levde i folkets mun,

och er bedrift levde i jordens sköte:
stenen bröts åter sönder och en ström
av livets vatten flöt ur glömd terräng.
Hästarna valde platsen för sitt möte.
Man minde sig om helgonens beröm:
era reliker restes från sin säng
mitt ibland springare som utan töm
och betsel njöt på paradisisk äng:
sanning blev nyfödd i en vacker dröm.

II (*till Gud Sonen*)

Vad var det för ett tempel Du, Gud, gjorde?
Blott ett beläte av Dig, inte mer?
Blott ett beläte av den Högste borde
räcka, men i dess tomhet steg Du ner.

Du sänkte Dig i stoffets mörka schakt
och nådde botten, krossades och dog.
Du dödde martyrdöden. Döden log.
Men martyrlivet levde kvar intakt.

Vad var det för en sten Du sprängde sönder?
Du sprängde sönder vår mållösa kropp:
avbröt eonens oberörda lopp:
återgav till oss straffnedtyngda bönder

vatten förutan spann, säd utan skära,
mjölk utan stallet, honung utan bien.
Allt kött är hö, men nu: hö utan lien.
Vår krassa intighet kom Du, Gud, nära.

Krass intighet gjorde Du full och öm:
Du öste ur Ditt väsen i fantomen.
Du rev Ditt hantverks mantel utan söm:
klöv Styx itu rakt under själapråmen:

Du stal allt ljus från glädjens himlavalv
och skänkte in det dit där vi begrät oss.
Förlåten rämnade och jorden skalv.
Förlåten rämnade och Du förlät oss.

III (*till människan och till Edens vaktande ångel*)

Den värld som är ett föremål för tro
och den som våra sinnen kan förnimma
binds samman av en mäktig andlig bro.
Verkstadens bud och verkets måste rimma.

Tål du nu, människa, den sortens rim?
Eller är allt som rimmar pekoral?
Är hymnen skrymtets eget tjo och tjim,
godtrogenheten olidligt banal?

Pecus är flocken, sinnesslö och trög –
nå, helgonkällan vattnade först djuren.
Före oss skapade Guds hand naturen.
Säg inte att Hans godkännande ljög.

Materien är mättad med mirakel.
Varje kvadrattum av varenda yta
döljer en helig kraft i stånd att bryta
seldonet loss från straffarbetets skakel.

I rättan tid skall Ordet återvända:
men marken här har redan börjat bäva.
Oförutsett kan varje kvark upphäva
lagarnas makt, och då får under hända.

Släpp fram oss nu, lustgårdens ordningsvakt.
Klädseln är fel, frisyrerna är trista,
att bröllopsfest stod på begrep vi sällan,
vi tog annonserna alltför abstrakt.
Låt inte sista räddningsplankan brista,
låt inte gammalt slarv komma emellan.
Här bjuds ett slut som ingen född vill mista:
släpp in oss i ikonen ut ur fällan!
Vänd bort eldsvärdets skoningslösa gnista!

Carmen Varangianum – A Song for the Varangian Martyrs

The tenth century protomartyrs of Russia, Saints Theodore and John of Kiev, commemorated on the twelfth (N.S. twenty-fifth) of July, were Varangians, i.e. of Scandinavian, almost certainly Swedish stock. The primary source of the story of the two saints is the Chronicle of Nestor, a monk of Kiev born in 1056.

The Varangians, East European equivalents of West Europe's Vikings, were of importance to the court at Constantinople as warriors and to the emerging Russian nation as tradesmen and providers of models for communal organization. The very name of Rus' or Russia is thought to derive from the *Ros* of Roslagen (the coastal area north of Stockholm). The early historical importance of Roslagen is seen in the fact that *Ros* has provided the Finnish word for Sweden, *Ruotsi*.

Sapphic strophe.

Carmen Nuptiale – Wedding Song

The story of the narriage at Cana is in John ii 1–10. Cf. also Eph. v 23–33. *Ecclesia*, church, is derived from the Greek verb ἐκκαλέω, to call forth.

The metre of this poem is that of Catullus's pagan wedding song lxi: three Catullan Glyconics with a refrain consisting of a Glyconic and a Pherecratean.

Narratio Sanctae Candidae – Saint Wite Tells her Tale

The English piece is the original and the Latin a paraphrase.

The relics of the Saxon martyr Saint Wite (or Candida) have – uniquely in Great Britain – been preserved since the Middle Ages in the parish church of Whitchurch Canonicorum in West Dorset. The flag mentioned in the poem, Saint Wite's Cross, was originally suggested by the author, received local support and was chosen to represent the county of Dorset in October 2008 after a poll among the public. It shows a white cross edged in red on a golden field.

The singular Galliambic metre is found in Catullus lxiii.

Dorsetiae Vexillum – Gold, Red and Silver: the Dorset Flag

The English piece is the original and the Latin a paraphrase. The flag is mentioned in the preceding poem. First Archilochian metre as in Horace's Ode IV vii.

Eleutheria – Freedom. The use of the Greek term will perhaps help to convey a sense of solemnity and momentousness. No

Sancta Candida cum vexillo nomine eius designato
maris ora sancta semper tumulique erant Deo

allusion is intended to particular religious or philosophical contexts in which it is found.

Carmen Matutinum – Morning Song
First Pythiambic system as in Horace's Epodes xiv, xv.

Carmen Athenis Peregrinati – Song of a Visitor to Athens
Fourth Archilochian metre as in Horace's Ode I iv.

In Fabulam Aliciae Prooemium – Prologue to a Story of Alice
This Latin version was made for the revised edition of *Alicia in Terra Mirabili* published by Evertype in 2011. Carroll's verse introduction can be found printed with the popular story. The English version here is a re-translation from the Latin.

Iambic trimeter acatalectic, in Horatian mode (e.g. Epode xvii) rather than Senecan.

Vespae Carmen – The Wasp's Song
A translation from lines (given here) written by Lewis Carroll for *Through the Looking-Glass* but together with the rest of the section concerning Alice's meeting with the wasp deleted before publication. This Latin version was made for the revised edition of *Aliciae per Speculum Transitus* which is to be published by Evertype.

Anapaestic dimeter, cf. Seneca's tragedies *passim*.

Minora – Short Pieces
CARMINIS SCHOLASTICI PARAPHRASIS LATINA – THE STATE OF HAPPINESS: This is a paraphrase (in Third Archilochian metre, cf. Horace's Epode xi) of a song written by the present author for Katarinaskolan, Uppsala, as a pastiche in an old form of Swedish:

Carmen Catharinaeum

Ur sanning födes glädje.
Sök sant, som glädjas vill.
Därom skolmästarn vädje.
Det lystre djäknen till.

Chara ex aletheias.
Hvarföre, huru, hvad,
spörj så, din själ befrias,
finn svar, hon blifver glad.

I leda går den late,
den trägne får behag.
Gör då *De veritate*
laetitia din lag.

PICAE – MAGPIES: hexameters.
PECCAVI – I HAVE SINNED: hexameters.
POËTA MAESTUS – THE POET DEJECTED: hexameters.
DROSERA – THE SUNDEW: the English piece is of course the original.
Hexameters.
DIANTHI BARBATI – SWEET WILLIAMS: Dianthus Barbatus is the botanical name of the garden flower known as Sweet William. These lines – possibly more sentimental than the facts would warrant – were written to honour the only brother of my maternal grandmother, Will Parsons, who was placed in a mental asylum at a young age, and his friend, Billy G., to whom he refers in a letter to my grandmother dated 27.10.(19)04. Elegiacs.

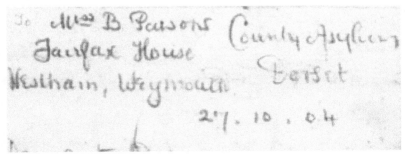

Please remember me to Billy G—
when you see him, he misses
his pal I expect.

Time goes very dull here, you know I shan't be
sorry when I shall have a change, but I
must be content, I suppose, and be thankful
I am keeping as well as I am. but its no
great catch to be shut up in one of these
places.

The Parsons family ca. 1902
Will, Nell, Frederick (father)
Bess, Allie, Emma (mother), Poll

SENIS SAPIENTIA – THE WISDOM OF AN OLD MAN: hexameter distich.
RARA AVIS – A RARE BIRD: trochaic tetrameter catalectic distich.
AD SENESCENTEM – TO SOMEONE GETTING OLD: hexameter distich.
AD DICTIONARIUM SUUM – TO HIS DICTIONARY (LEWIS AND SHORT):
  hexameter distich.
ΕΙΣ ΤΗΝ ΑΛΗΘΕΙΑΝ ΥΜΝΟΣ ΕΥΡΩΠΑΙΟΣ (AD VERITATEM HYMNUS
  EUROPAEUS) – TO TRUTH: A HYMN FOR EUROPE: trochaic tetrameter
  catalectic.

The aim was to provide a Latin (and thus supranational) text in an authentic metre (that of the Pervigilium Veneris) which can be sung to Beethoven's melody for Schiller's An die Freude. Two versions have been provided, one, more "classical", without rhyme, and another with the rhyming which many prefer.

The new text needed to be relevant to the ideals of Europeans of the present day and, as far as can be judged, those of the future; neither specifically religious nor non-religious; of the same general type as Schiller's but with the mythological pretence played down.

A text in Greek would have been less usable than one in Latin, but the title in Greek will show deference to the older culture and may somewhat alleviate misgivings concerning Latin on the part of Greeks and other Orthodox Europeans.

Any accepted pronunciation of the Latin can be used, but I suggest the choral-Italian for singing, since then the length of syllables will in any case not be felt and the effect of a piece of mediaeval rhymed writing will come to the fore. In such a context the title could be read with either classical or modern Greek pronunciation. However when the text is simply read aloud I suggest classical pronunciation and attention to the length of syllables.

Epigrammata Scholastica Selecta – Selected School Epigrams

Classes at Katarinaskolan, Uppsala, are assigned animals and birds as names and symbols to be shown on heraldic shields. Elegiac distichs.

Repraesentatio insignium heraldicorum ab auctore in Suetia
adhibitorum: sed secundum verba haicus
Tellure nullum repperimus comitem ducemque nullum.

Haicua – Haikus Translated

See Metrical Innovation, p. 199 below.

Carmina Tria Stilo Mediaevali Confecta – Three Songs in Mediaeval Style

CANTUS FESTIVUS DE SANCTA CATHARINA – FEAST DAY SONG FOR SAINT
  CATHERINE: in Latin with refrain in Greek. The author has
  provided this song with a tune in a Latin-American rhythm to
  which it is sung with gusto towards the end of November at
  Katarinaskolan, Uppsala.

CARMEN NATALICIUM SALVATORIS – A GRAIL CAROL: the Latin stanzas
  are a paraphrase from a song originally written in English with a
  Latin refrain:

A Grail Carol
A Christmas Song for the Earth

See, this world of ours, all dark and frozen,
is the vessel that the Lord has chosen
to receive the gift of blood and water
flowing from our Saviour's wounded side.
Thus He makes the earth His Son's sole bride,
saves her life and takes her for His daughter.
Benedictus ...

Eve, a rib from Adam's side transmuted,
is the ground wherein our stock is rooted:
now on Mary's branch the Lord of Ages
grafts a Bud of everlasting bloom.
Mingled lifesap falls on Adam's tomb
and his bones' impatient thirst assuages.

Since that Eve, though night delayed our waking,
prophets sang a star to sign dawn's breaking:
now at last the Sun of Justice rises,
blessing with His dew the fevered air:
and where Rachel died her babe to bear
Mary wins us life, most dear of prizes.

Christ the True Vine joins our barren number,
first-fruit of a race in clayey slumber,
staked and pruned, harsh torment undergoing
till the world's elixir be distilled.
Cana's wedding-cups with wine are filled;
creatures all with grace are overflowing.

CANDIDA CREVISTI – SHINING WHITE: see the note on Narratio
Sanctae Candidae – Saint Wite Tells her Tale *supra*.

In Where Dorset meets Devon, London 1911, Francis Bickley,
having recounted the discovery of Saint Wite's bones, writes: "There
was formerly a painted inscription on the front of the tomb. This is
now entirely lost, and within man's memory nothing has been
decipherable except

> *CANDIDA* ...
> *CANDIDIORQUE* ...

Now it takes no great erudition to see that this is the truncation of
an elegiac couplet." Bickley offers a reconstruction:

> *Candida mundanis olim vivebat in aulis.*
> *Candidiorque nitens vivit in aede Dei.*

Bickley's translation of his couplet is this:

> *Once white in worldly palaces she trod:*
> *whiter she shineth in the house of God.*

However this wording takes for granted a nineteenth century
identification of Saint Wite with the Breton princess Saint Gwen –
an identification now realized to be impossible since it conflicts with
the unequivocal ecclesiastical tradition that Saint Wite was martyred.
Taking Bickley's example as a challenge I composed a distich which
is in accord with the tradition:

> *Candida crevisti manibus moritura malorum:*
> *candidiorque capis praemia plena polo.*

A literal English equivalent: *Shining white you grew up, destined to die at the hands of evil men: and even more shining white you receive full rewards in heaven.* Soon afterwards I added rhyming echoes to the four sections of my distich and put it to music as the last in a set of Dorset songs.

For *polus* in the sense of the heaven of Christian faith rather than the visible sky cf. Prudentius' Peristephanon ii 552, where Saint Laurence is praised for having a twofold dwelling, that of the body being here, that of the mind being in heaven: *est aula nam duplex tibi, hic corporis, mentis polo.*

METRICAL INNOVATION

It would be surprising had a modern practitioner of Latin verse not written in dactylic hexameters and elegiacs and in other metres and strophic patterns found in the works of Horace, Catullus and Seneca. Where such as these are to hand they have been named in the preceding Notes on the Poems.

The metrical systems I myself have introduced are to a large extent novel combinations of verse rhythms known to antiquity. In such verses I have generally not disregarded established practice regarding the placing of caesuras. Exceptions can be seen in *Fragmenta Mythica*, where the expected caesuras are occasionally missing in the Lesser Sapphic and Phalaecean verses, and in the first part of *Extemporalia ante Ver Inceptum* in a couple of iambic trimeter catalectic verses.

The few distinctly innovative verse rhythms in my poetry will not really need designations of their own unless or until they are the subject of wider discussion; however I have amused myself by inventing names and using them in these metrical notes. (Here b = *brevis*, short; l = *longa*, long, a = *anceps*, short or long.)

Greater Ionodactylic
b b l l | b b l l | l b b l b a   Urbes

Lesser Ionodactylic
b b l l | b b l b a   *Urbes, An Velut Carmen*

Mixophalaecean
l b l b l l l b b l a   *Fragmenta mythica, Extemporalia I*

It should be noted that an acceptable system cannot be composed of entirely disparate rhythmic elements. In a four-verse strophe I find that usually three verses together, or each of two separate pairs of verses, should have some clearly audible coherence.

A. In the initial Mixophalaecean verse of the strophe of the first part of *Extemporalia* the sound of the opening trochees *l b l b* reflects the basic *b l b l* etc. of the iambic verses, while its spondee and dactyl have a similarity to the two dactyls or spondee-plus-dactyl of the fourth verse.

B. In the four-verse components of the system of *Fragmenta Mythica* (see below) both coherence and variety are provided by the fact that the first three verses each consist of different orderings of three elements, namely two trochees and a spondee-dactyl combination, together with a final spondee or trochee. The last six syllables of the fourth verse (iambic trimeter catalectic) are the same as those of the Phalaecean.

C. In *De Non Haesitante Amore Meditatio Vespertina* the dactylic hexameters and Greater Archilochians are made always to begin with a spondee followed by a dactyl, thus providing a judicious degree of homogeneity with the other two verses of the strophe (a Lesser Asclepiadean and a Phalaecean). In this system moreover the last six syllables of the Greater Archilochian echo the last six of the Phalaecean.

D. In other systems coherence is often evident from the names of the metres represented. The Greater Archilochian verse, it will be remembered, is nothing other than a juxtaposition of dactylic and trochaic sequences.

Metres in practice

1. In *Onyx Nardi* the spondee does not replace the first iambus of the iambic trimeters and dimeters: this in order to provide relief from the heavily spondaic openings of the other two verses in the strophe.

2. *Mustela vel potius Telamus* – After a brief introductory passage in elegiacs and another in First Pythiambics (alternating dactylic hexameter and iambic dimeter acatalectic) the poem is written in tetrastichs of iambic trimeter acatalectic. In these, as in *Ad Ingratos Datores* and *In Fabulam Aliciae Prooemium* (for this poem see also 4.) I have followed precedent in allowing not only spondees but also anapaests and dactyls frequently to be substituted in the odd-numbered feet, and tribrachs in the second and fourth feet.

3. In the first and second parts of *Extemporalia* and also in *Icon Sanctorum Flori et Lauri* the first dactyl of the dactylic hemipentameter has at times been replaced by a spondee.

4. *Scaena Brahmsiana* – In the iambic trimeter acatalectic verses I have allowed a tribrach in the second foot of verse 15 and in the first foot of verse 28. For the use of a tribrach in the first foot of the iambic trimeter (also in verses 30 and 33 of *In Fabulam Aliciae Prooemium*) see Horace Epode xi 27.

5. With the exception of *Mustela vel potius Telamus, In Fabulam Aliciae Prooemium* and the two already mentioned verses of *Scaena Brahmsiana* my practice in iambic verses has been not to admit any substitutions except that of spondees in odd-numbered feet. (In the first part of *Vox Ter Cupida*, entitled Puer, the even-numbered verses are purely iambic, following the example of Horace Epode xvi.)

6. *In Fabulam Aliciae Prooemium* and *Carmen Matutinum* – When in these pieces the opportunity is taken to present texts in groups of respectively seven and six verses, which happens not to be unfeasible with regard to the structure of the texts, this is done so that the eye shall be attracted rather than to suggest that a strophic structure ought to be felt by the reader.

Strophic Systems

Urbes
> Iambic trimeter catalectic
> Greater Ionodactylic
> Iambic trimeter catalectic
> Lesser Ionodactylic

Occasiones Servatae
> Greater Archilochian
> Iambic trimeter catalectic
> Iambic trimeter acatalectic
> Dactylic hemipentameter

Fragmenta Mythica – twelve-verse systems (each verse containing eleven syllables) composed of the following four-verse pattern repeated:

Lesser Sapphic	*l b l l l b b l b l a*
Phalaecean ("hendecasyllable")	*l l l b b l b l b l a*
Mixophalaecean	*l b l b l l l b b l a*
Iambic trimeter catalectic	*... l b l b l a*

Mustela vel potius Telamus consists mainly of tetrastichs of iambic trimeter acatalectic: see 2. above.

Onyx Nardi
>Lesser Asclepiadean
>Iambic trimeter acatalectic
>Greater Asclepiadean
>Iambic dimeter acatalectic

Extemporalia ante Ver Inceptum I
>Mixophalaecean
>Iambic trimeter catalectic
>Iambic trimeter catalectic
>Dactylic hemipentameter (see 3. above)

Extemporalia ante Ver Inceptum II
>Iambic trimeter acatalectic
>Iambic dimeter calalectic
>Iambic trimeter acatalectic
>Dactylic hemipentameter (see 3. above)

Extemporalia ante Ver Inceptum III
>Dactylic hexameter
>Iambic trimeter acatalectic
>Iambic trimeter catalectic
>Dactylic hemipentameter

De Non Haesitante Amore Meditatio Vespertina (see C. above)
Dactylic hexameter (here:)   *l l l b b l ...*
Lesser Asclepiadean   *l l l b b l ...*
Phalaecean   *l l l b b l b l b l a*
Greater Archilochian (here:)   *l l l b b l ... l b l b l a*

Scaena Brahmsiana (see 4. above) – mostly the following four-verse strophe, but with interspersed three-verse groups of Greater Asclepiadeans:
    Iambic trimeter acatalectic
    Anapaestic dimeter catalectic (cf. Ausonius IV xvii)
    Iambic trimeter acatalectic
    Iambic dimeter calalectic

An Velut Carmen – in the final strophe three trochaic tetrameter catalectic verses stand in place of the single one:
    Lesser Sapphic   *l b l l l ...*
    Trochaic tetrameter catalectic   *l b l a l ... l b l a l ...*
    Lesser Sapphic   *l b l l l ...*
    Lesser Ionodactylic

Simul Evidentia atque Obscura – Cretic tetrameters with diaeresis between the second and third feet, arranged in tetrastichs. I allow other feet of five morae to replace cretics: bacchii and fourth paeons in all positions and antibacchii and first paeons in all except the last foot of a verse. As usual the final syllable of any verse is treated as anceps.

Icon Sanctorum Flori et Lauri – a four-verse strophe of mixed iambodactylic character, cf. Horace's Epodes xi and xiii–xvi. Here however the system is more complex than those used by Horace. The first verse combines the first 2½ feet of a dactylic hexameter (equivalent to a dactylic hemipentameter but allowing spondees in both the first and the second feet) with an iambic dimeter; the second an iambic dimeter with the remaining 3½ feet of the hexameter (i.e. with an anapaestic dimeter catalectic, see *Scaena Brahmsiana* above). The third verse is an iambic trimeter hypercatalectic (cf. the third verse of Horace's Alcaic strophe which is most simply understood as a form of iambic dimeter hyper-catalectic: for my use of substitutions see note 2. above on iambic trimeter acatalectic verses) and the fourth verse is a dactylic hemipentameter as noted in 3. above.

Haikus

If around the time Horace was writing the iambodactylic epodes the suggestion had been made that he should write minuscule poems with verses of five, seven and five syllables – well, the hypothesis must seem ridiculously unlikely. But we can pretend that he might have decided to try a familiar iambic sequence in the first and third verses, and an equally familiar dactylic in the middle verse:

a l b l a
l b b l b b a
a l b l a

Ingram Content Group UK Ltd.
Milton Keynes UK
UKHW020935100423
419912UK00008B/22